THE PEARL IS IN THE OYSTER

To my love

Marj

from Bob

8-20-81

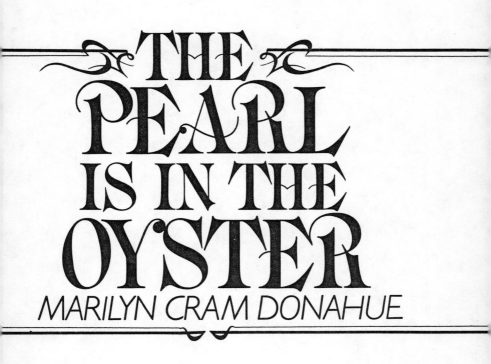

THE PEARL IS IN THE OYSTER

MARILYN CRAM DONAHUE

Tyndale House
Publishers, Inc.
Wheaton, Illinois

Library of Congress
Catalog Card Number
79–66809
ISBN 0–8423–4808–5,
paper
First printing, April 1980
Printed in the United States
of America.

TO BOB
who helped me learn the value
of a pearl

CONTENTS

ACKNOWLEDGMENTS

Portions of this book have been published previously in various periodicals. Grateful acknowledgment is given to the publishers for permission to reprint this material.

"Please Don't Smash the Rubber Elephants," in *Guideposts,* Copyright 1978 by Guideposts Associates, Inc., Carmel, New York 10512.

"Beauty There For The Seeing," in *Farm Wife News,* copyright 1978, The Farm Wife, Inc.

"The Silkspinners," in *Scope,* copyright 1978, Augsburg Publishing House.

"Let Your Knots Hang Loose," in *Power For Living,* copyright 1978, Scripture Press Publications, Inc., Wheaton, Ill. 60187.

"Hang Loose," in *Today's Christian Parent,* copyright autumn 1978, The Standard Publishing Co.

"The Eye Of The Wind," in *Insight,* a Christian youth magazine published by Seventh-day Adventists, copyright 1979, Review and Herald Publishing Association, Washington, D.C. 20012.

"The Waiting Game," in *Scope,* copyright 1978, Augsburg Publishing House.

"Rural Reflections," in *Farm Wife News,* copyright 1978, The Farm Wife, Inc.

INTRODUCTION
ONIONS, PEARLS, AND PROMISES

. . . the kingdom of heaven is like a merchant in search of fine pearls, who, on finding one pearl of great value, went and sold all that he had and bought it.
Matthew 13:45, 46

This morning I peeled an onion. Under my sharp knife the skin came away easily, like crisp brown paper, revealing the shiny surface beneath. I cut the whole thing in half and laid the two pieces on the chopping board. It was then that I noticed the layers, fitting tightly, one against the other, smooth and round, as if the whole thing had been dipped, like a candle, into thick layers of hot wax.

Oh, I'd known for a long time how onions were put together. I hadn't made a new discovery, or anything like that. It's just that I took a second look this morning . . . because I had been thinking of pearls.

That's right . . . pearls. The kind you wear around your neck. Translucent gems. Those shiny little beads that grow in oysters. A strange comparison? Not really. A cut pearl is a little like a sliced onion, you know. Or maybe you didn't know . . . that it's formed in layers, one tightly wrapped around the other. There, thankfully, the resemblance ends.

An onion is an onion. Nothing more; nothing less. But a pearl is proof that beauty can exist deep in the heart of a roughened exterior. A gem of great value, it is unique, like the human soul, for no two pearls are ever the same. Sometimes an imitation can be mistaken for the real thing, but not for long. If you peel off the lustrous layers, you'll see that they're made of nothing but powdered fish scales hiding a bead of glass.

What on earth does all this have to do with you and me? A great deal, because, believe it or not, that's the way you're made too . . . in layers. Have you taken a good look lately? Step right up to the mirror. What do you see? A reflection, of course. A picture of the outer you. So far, so good, but you haven't gone quite far enough.

Whether you like it or not, a good deal of the inner you is showing. The way you feel; the way you think; your happiness and your discontent . . . these things are as much a part of your appearance as the shape of your nose and the curve of your face.

Paints and perfumes cover up a lot. They can enhance and improve. But they're concerned entirely with your outer shell. They don't provide that inner glow that sets some people . . . and some pearls . . . apart from others.

Commercial beauty is a multimillion-dollar business. Open a magazine and read the ads. It's possible to paint, tint, pluck, and cream yourself into an outer vision of loveliness, but as long as you can wipe it off at night, or dissolve it before it chips, you're dealing with the outer layer, not the genuine article.

Now don't get me wrong. There's nothing the matter with wanting to look your best. It's hard to feel good inside when you know you're a mess. I once knew a wise woman who said, "When you wake up in the morning

and everything looks dim, get up and dress up. It lifts
your spirits faster than any other remedy.''

So go right ahead and pamper the physical you. Feed
it; clothe it; make sure it looks its best. After all, you live
in that body. How you treat it is important, because it
houses the other you, and it does get the work done.

But don't forget to take a good long look under the
skin. That's where your natural resources are, and they
have to be developed from the inside out. That's the way
a pearl is made . . . from the inside out. Its luster doesn't
come from surface shininess. It comes from layer after
layer of rich translucence, formed a little at a time: a living
process of development and change. No powdered fish
scales. No cheap bead of glass.

That's what this book is all about. It's the irritant—the
grain of sand, if you like—that will get the process under-
way. I believe, you see, that God meant for each one of
us to be beautiful. We are supposed to take whatever we
were given to work with and stretch it until it reaches a
new dimension. The idea is to end up more like a pearl
than an onion. And not an imitation either. What you're
aiming for is the real thing.

The trouble is, when we look inside, we find that our
natural resources are sadly underdeveloped. So where do
we go from there? We need some guidelines, some clear,
explicit statements. We need to know exactly what our
inner layers need to be made of if we're going to shine.

Somebody already told us. Years ago, a Man climbed a
hill and spoke of the qualities of character which make
people blessed, or happy. He listed them one by one,
simply and clearly. Today we call them the Beatitudes.
They are so familiar to most of us that we read them
without thinking about what they mean.

The words are beautiful, full of rhythm and life. They
speak of human experiences, of potential, of promised
happiness. That much we know for sure. What we don't
understand is *how* and *why?* Even though they are

simple, straightforward statements, they are not easy to understand. Who really wants to be poor in spirit? What could be the possible advantage of hunger? To be tested by sorrow doesn't sound to me like any fun at all.

Can these things really make us happy inside? Can they build the layers of character that make us more beautiful, more blessed human beings? It must be so, because Jesus was a practical man. He spoke to the multitudes, and his lessons were meant to be applied. But he gave no easy answers. He planted seeds. It's up to us to harvest the crop.

We come to know what the Beatitudes mean, not by reciting the words like well-loved nursery rhymes, but by confronting the challenges of daily living; by reacting to joys and sorrows; by building, layer upon layer, our personal pearls. Happiness, you see, is a product of being and doing . . . not of waiting and expecting. That was the secret Jesus wanted to share.

Although perfect pearls are rare, they're not impossible to find. And they're well worth all the trouble. Reach in now, and plant the tiny seed . . . the irritant that makes the whole process work. Then watch your own pearl grow, chapter by chapter, as you turn the pages of this book.

ONE
BUTTERFLY
ON YOUR FINGERTIP

Blessed are the poor in spirit, for theirs is the kingdom of heaven.   Matthew 5:3

When was the last time you were down in the dumps? Remember how it was? You couldn't seem to do anything right. You were unhappy with yourself and everybody else. Your heart was heavy; your spirits sagged. In short, you had the blues.

We've all been like that, and it's nothing to crow about. It's downright depressing to be so painfully aware of your own poverty. Now don't raise your eyebrows when I say that word. Your bank account may be in fine shape. You may have all the bills paid and a new car in the driveway. But you know perfectly well that's not what I'm talking about. When you're poor in spirit, you're poverty stricken in the worst kind of way. There's something important missing from your life, and you can't put your finger on what it is. You're probably sure of one thing. At this particular moment, you don't feel especially blessed.

It's pretty hard to feel happy when there's a dark cloud hanging over your head. But wait a minute! Dark clouds do have a way of moving on. They don't hang around forever, and that's a fact. Storms come and go. I'll admit that they create a little havoc, but they also do a pretty good job of clearing the air. It happens that way with the weather, and it happens the same way with you. At the risk of sounding trite, let me tell you something. There *is* a silver lining on the edge of that cloud.

Just when you think everything is darkest, someone or something always happens along and brightens your day. If you haven't noticed, you must have been going through life with your eyes closed. Be honest now. Try to remember the times you've said things like: "What would I do without you?" "All I needed was a good laugh!" "Thanks for dropping by and cheering me up." How often have you crawled out of bed on the wrong side, then, halfway through the day, realized that things were looking up?

My friend Julie has three teenage daughters. "Sometimes," she confides, "I think they live on a teeter-totter. Life for them is a series of ups and downs. The only thing that keeps me going is the knowledge that the downs won't last forever."

I have news for Julie. Teenagers don't have a priority on seesaws. *Life* is a series of ups and downs. Jesus understood this. He knew that each one of us has our bad days, our times of being *down*hearted, *down*-in-the-mouth, *down*-in-the-dumps. He also knew that it doesn't last forever. If we just hang in there, something eventually happens to turn our lives right side up again.

Let me tell you another fact. There's no permanent cure. Only a robot can avoid being poor in spirit *every* now and then. Things do happen in our lives that make us sad.

Those Happy Hatties who go around always wearing ear-to-ear smiles aren't necessarily any more blessed than the rest of us, and I'll tell you why. They view life as a giant toothpaste ad. They're afraid to let themselves feel, because they know that if they put one foot in the water, they're liable to get wet. We've all known people like that . . . afraid to run, because they might fall; afraid to try, because they might fail; afraid to live, because they might die. They're happy on the outside, but that's as far as it goes.

Jesus wasn't talking about finding a happy corner to hide in. He was talking about *living*, about trying and failing and trying again. He was talking about the glimpses of truth and beauty that make it all worthwhile. Call *those*, if you will, the kingdom of heaven. But don't let the words scare you. They don't mean you're coming face to face with brass bands and royal purple.

Remember that Jesus spoke of God as a Father, not a sceptered monarch. So, to be part of the kingdom of heaven is not to stand before a golden throne, but instead, to be a child of God . . . to know the peace and beauty of belonging. Don't think of the kingdom of heaven as just a shining city on some far-off cloud. It's also within you. He said it himself.

An elderly friend once said to me, "Think of heaven, and your mind goes up." She laughed when I automatically looked at the ceiling. "I'm not talking about direction, as much as quality," she protested.

The kingdom of heaven is like treasure hidden in a field, which a man found and covered up; then in his joy he goes and sells all that he has and buys that field.
                                                     Matthew 13:44

Did you see that key word? JOY! The kingdom of heaven brings an upsurge of joy. It comes as a gift, by God's grace, and it comes when we need it most. In unexpected moments.

It doesn't have to be something earthshaking. Don't expect to see flashing lights and hear celestial music. At least, that's not what turns the key and opens the door for me. It's usually a simple thing. Something as natural as friendship, or a sunrise . . . both miracles of a kind. Something that steals up quietly and unexpectedly and fills my heart with wonder. It can be as common a thing as a smile. It can weigh as little as a butterfly. And it can be shared. Joy is a little like a box of candy. Once the lid is lifted, everyone can have a taste.

Let me tell you a story about someone I once knew. Mildred Glover was poor in spirit. There was no doubt about it. She was absolutely poverty stricken. But something happened one day. It was only a little miracle, but it changed her life, and in so doing it scattered a little gold dust on a tarnished spot in mine.

It was a July afternoon, hot and sticky, and Mildred was complaining again. "I can hardly breathe," she panted. She leaned over the railing at the side of the ship, as if she hoped to find the air cooler there. "I should never have come," she told anyone who would listen. "This trip is ruining my health."

"Her health is ruining my trip," my husband whispered. Several others nodded in agreement. We were all, literally, in the same boat, traveling at a snail's pace through the Panama Canal in less than ideal weather. The only real problem was Mildred. Her constant complaints were beginning to make everyone uncomfortable.

"Why don't you go inside for awhile?" I suggested. "It's air-conditioned, and you can see quite well through the long windows."

She scowled at me as if I'd told her to jump overboard. "I don't want to go inside," she snapped. "I don't want to miss anything." Her face turned red, and her harsh voice rose to an alarming pitch. "I paid my money, and I want it all!" She waved one hand dramatically at the scenery. Her forefinger was pointed, as if ready to pick out the details that she was claiming for her own.

Suddenly she stopped, her arm outstretched. A look of surprise, almost of pain, crossed her face. Her lips moved, but there was no sound. I reached out toward her, thinking she must really be ill, but my husband caught my hand and held it. "Look!" he said.

A small yellow butterfly, its wings opening and closing in slow motion, had come to rest on the very tip of her outstretched finger. She didn't move, but the butterfly did, turning around on delicate legs and warming itself in the tropical sun.

"Catch it," someone suggested. "Press it in a book, and take it home for a souvenir."

The look she gave him was something I'll always remember: an expression of sadness, because she knew something that he couldn't possibly understand. Mildred, the woman with the voice that wouldn't quit, shook her head and whispered softly, "Why me?"

At that instant I remembered a summer day, years ago, when I was a child. We waited eagerly every year for the appearance of the first butterflies, especially the graceful swallowtails. There was a special game we played. If we could just capture the first swallowtail and hold it in our hands, summer would last forever. One particular morning we ran after one of the creatures, our bare feet padding on the warming grass, our hands reaching high, our fingertips coaxing.

The butterfly always escaped, lifting out of reach with its slow-motioned flutter. Finally someone remembered the net. Excitement grew until . . . at last . . . the crucial moment came, and the butterfly was caught in a manmade web. What next? We tried to turn it loose, but we had damaged its wings, and it couldn't fly. It struggled, but it was no use. One of the boys thought a quick ending would be most merciful, so he arranged it: a long, sharp pin through its heart. But it didn't die. It lived all day, one of God's most graceful creatures, still struggling against our thoughtlessness.

As a child I sat in the grass and cried. As a woman I stood on the deck and saw the sadness in Mildred's eyes. I, too, had known something that the others didn't understand: that there are some things that can't be captured and placed, like trophies, in glass cases. Those are the things that come as gifts, with no strings attached and for no apparent reason. But for me the knowledge had come too late, for my butterfly was dead.

I watched Mildred with something like envy until she turned to me and smiled. "I feel as if someone had pried open a rough oyster and shown me the pearl inside," she said. To my amazement, I felt exactly the same way. It was as if I could reach out my own hand and feel Mildred's butterfly on the tip of my finger.

We stayed on the deck a long time. At last, the butterfly spread its wings and gracefully flew away. I watched it until it was out of sight.

"Amazing grace," I thought, in the words of the old hymn. God's grace *is* a lot like a butterfly. It can't be bought or captured with a net. It comes instead at unexpected moments and rests quietly, like a second chance, fluttering softly on your fingertip . . . a thing of beauty and an offering of God's love. God's grace, I knew now, was meant to be shared. For Mildred's butterfly had touched me too.

By the next morning, Mildred was complaining again, but now her words were good-natured, and her tongue didn't bite. She never spoke of what had happened, but there was definitely something different about her because of it.

I rejoiced for her, and I rejoiced for myself. I wonder if she ever realized that the butterfly on her fingertip had set my butterfly free.

Sometimes being poor spirited, you see, is more than a twenty-four-hour malady. It's something we carry around hidden deep within us, even when we outwardly laugh and love and carry on the routines of daily living. It's more than a case of the blues. It can be a sorrow, a deep regret, a bad memory. It can be a thing we have buried deep and seldom uncover, but which is, nevertheless, a drain on our spiritual resources . . . a tiny microbe which pollutes the spring of the water of life.

Even then, perhaps especially then, when we are old

friends to heartache and sadness, we become fertile ground for seeds of faith. Mildred Glover was a contentious woman. She was chronically poor in spirit. Quite possibly she did nothing to deserve her butterfly, but it came anyway, in a moment of graceful beauty.

The miracle is always twofold. First, when you have wept for the poverty of yourself, you can better appreciate the joy of newfound riches. Second, the joy that you feel can't be contained. It spreads like melted butter, over the people around you.

Your experiences won't always be as dramatic as Mildred's, but they'll be just as important.

The kingdom of heaven is like a grain of mustard seed which a man took and sowed in his field; it is the smallest of all seeds, but when it has grown it is the greatest of shrubs and becomes a tree, so that the birds of the air come and make nests in its branches.

Matthew 13:31, 32

Learn to accept those special moments. Accept them gratefully. There are no strings attached. Plant them in the soil of your heart. Then feel your joy grow.

Remember this! There is nothing poor-spirited about a butterfly. But it can be elusive if you try to chase it. It comes as a gift, and this is what God's grace is all about. It is a gift, and it is a promise. Because you have taken a chance on life, because you have taken your turn with despair, you will appreciate the butterfly moments. A wise man once told me: "Of course the sunrise is beautiful, but it wouldn't be half as lovely if it didn't come at the end of darkness."

This is what Jesus was talking about. He was promising the silver lining. He was telling us not to be afraid. He was offering the gift of living, with all the risks that are involved. But he was also assuring us that there is help along the way. Isn't that what faith is all about? It's what keeps us from giving up the ship. It's the knowledge that no matter how badly we feel, there's a better day around the corner.

In the meantime, look at living as a challenge. That's how you form the first lustrous layer of the pearl that is growing inside of you. There's only one word of warning. Don't ever become so involved with your own pearl that you crawl inside the shell. Remember to spread a little of that joy around. The next time you feel full of happiness, reach out your hand and set someone else's butterfly free.

Here's how to polish the first precious layer of your pearl:

1. Take time every day to listen to someone. Try to hear more than the sound of a voice. Care! And let that person know it.

2. Do something unnecessary. Something beyond the call of duty. It can be as simple as a candied cherry on top of a pale pudding or a surprise phone call to a friend. Let your heart be warmed by the smile that results.

3. Stop whatever you're doing and take a moment to be aware of how good you feel. Say to yourself, "The kingdom of heaven is within me. I know it, and I'm glad."

4. When you have a series of poor spirited days, and you begin to wonder if your cloud *does* have a silver lining, take a tip from Scarlett O'Hara. Remember that there's always a tomorrow, and it will be here sooner than you think.

5. If you get tired of waiting, read these words:

Happiness is like a butterfly.
The more you chase it, the more it will elude you.
But if you turn your attention to other things,
It comes and sits softly on your shoulder.

L. Richard Lessor

Thank you, Father,
for the gift of your kingdom,
for the melody of sunshine
drying the earth after a storm.
Give us the grace to accept
your gifts. . . .
Let us lift our hearts and rejoice
in the butterflies that you send
to tremble at our fingertips.

TWO
DON'T SMASH THE RUBBER ELEPHANTS

*Blessed are those who mourn, for they shall be
comforted.*   Matthew 5:4

Fortunately, human beings were born with tear ducts.
So were a lot of animals, but *our* tear ducts were intend-
ed for more than lubrication. The ability to weep is, as far
as I know, a uniquely human trait, an expression of
sorrow that removes our defenses and allows an outward
expression of grief.

What's so great about that? Wouldn't the world be
better without any grief at all? Possibly. But that's not the
way it is. Sorrow, whether you like it or not, is a fact of
life. It was Byron who said, "Ah, surely nothing dies but
something mourns." It's as natural as breathing, and just
as necessary—*if* you're going to be a sensitive, compas-
sionate human being.

Remember the age-old question that adults love to ask
little children: "Johnny, what are you going to be when
you grow up?" It's a harmless enough game we play. It
might even put a bee in Johnny's bonnet and help him
think about his future. But we don't let it go at that. At
the very same time we're urging Johnny to think about

growing up, we're also handing him a handkerchief and telling him to wipe his eyes, because big boys don't cry.

Let me tell you something. A child who is denied tears grows up to become an adult who can't express his feelings. When we deny ourselves one of our basic and most natural capabilities, we play a dangerous game. It leads to anger, frustration, and ulcers. It makes unhappiness a one-way street.

Jesus doesn't tell us not to mourn. On the contrary! He applauds our ability to feel sorrow. It's evidence of our humanity, and it's something he shared with us. One of the most dramatic statements in the New Testament is composed of only two words: "Jesus wept" (John 11:35). He felt things deeply. He was involved in life. He expected no less from the rest of us.

Once I overheard a conversation in the supermarket. Two women were pushing their shopping carts side by side. "Marian," said the first woman, "I know you're upset, but you've got to stop letting this thing bother you. You have to learn to be a little thick skinned about life."

Marian stopped and looked her companion in the eye. "If God had wanted me to be thick skinned," she replied, "he would have given me the hide of an alligator."

I never found out what "this thing" was. I wasn't even interested. What intrigued me was Marian's unique ability to acknowledge her humanity. She was a woman who was committed to living—with her defenses *down*. Let's face it: nobody enjoys being hurt. If we knew how to avoid all the pitfalls of life, we probably would. But we don't. So if we're anything like Marian we jump right in with both feet and take our chances.

Sure, we're going to suffer losses. Sometimes we'll feel pain, but how much better it is to jump in with both feet than to perch cowering on the diving board.

Let me tell you about Sarah Aldrich. When I went to visit her recently, the first thing I saw was the brilliant display of yellow tree roses lining her front walk. They grew tall and strong and filled the air with their midsummer sweetness. I reached out my hand to hold one in my palm, wanting to feel its softness against my skin . . . and remembered to be careful just in time. These were old-fashioned roses, the sweetest kind, but not thorn free. As a child, I'd often reached out to pick one and always come away wounded. So I touched the petals gently, left the flower on the bush, and moved on to the front door.

Sarah was an elderly woman, a family friend of long standing. Because of the miles between us, I hadn't seen her for some time. She was living alone for the first time in over fifty years. I knew that the loss of her husband had been devastating. I also knew that she had gone through a difficult period of mourning.

Yet here she was today, the picture of health, greeting me with a smile. We went into the house, where she had laid a small table with tiny iced cakes. The smell of fresh mint tea rose from the white china pot, curling upward in fragrant, steamy trails.

We sat and sipped and talked of small, but well-remembered things. Sarah didn't speak of herself until I was ready to leave. We went outside and stood in the afternoon air, heavy with the fragrance of her roses. She reached out and snapped off a fresh young bud and handed it to me. I saw the tiny drop of blood on her finger where a thorn had pricked it.

"You've hurt yourself!" I exclaimed.

She looked at the spot and wiped it clean. "It's not the first time, and probably not the last." There was a moment of silence. Then she spoke hesitantly, as if she were about to share something special.

"Look at that flower," she said. "You can take it apart if you want to and count the petals, each one soft and sweet. You can count the thorns too, if you're so inclined. There's nothing soft about those.

"The game of life is a good deal like a rose bush," she went on. "It has its share of thorns. If you're going to play the game without gloves, you'll probably bleed a little, but you'll also be able to feel the soft touch of the rose. That's something I wouldn't want to miss."

She turned and went into the house. But I stood a moment, looking at the soft yellow bud she had placed in my hand. Sarah had said that I could count the petals, but I didn't have to. I could see for myself that the flower at the end of the stem was well worth the thorns along the way.

The game of life was a winning game for Sarah Aldrich. She'd worked her problems out, reaching for comfort and receiving it. Her faith had sustained her. Like Marian, she was willing to live with her defenses down.

This may come as a shocker . . . but all people don't work that way. Some need a little outside help. Unlike Marian and Sarah, they are unable to jump off the diving board. Their defenses are up, and they're stuck tight.

This is where the rest of us come into the picture. If you think the second Beatitude is a platitude, you'd better read it again. It's a direct challenge, and it's directed at you and at me.

Comfort is the key word. It means more than solace. It means more than a drying of tears. It means an offer of strength and hope. Here's the big question. Where's it coming from?

"From God!" you exclaim. "Where else?" Well, you're right. But that's not all there is to it. God works in many ways, often through us. If you would be comforted in *your* time of need, you must be willing to pass on strength and hope to someone else.

I can remember a summer, years ago, when all four of our children had mumps at the same time. They recovered, then promptly contracted measles. When things were at their worst, my neighbor, Ruth, came to the door bringing our dinner. I was overwhelmed. "How can I ever thank you?" I asked.

"Don't," was her reply. "But here's what you *can* do.

The very first chance you get, do as much for someone
else. The next chance you get, do it again."

What a wonderful way to become involved with each
other—by multiple actions instead of single deeds!

"No man is an island." John Donne said it first, and
we've been paraphrasing it ever since. We are irretrieva-
bly involved with each other. Don't you see what this
means? It means that mourning for yourself and *receiving*
comfort is not enough. You have to mourn for others and
offer whatever strength comes from your personal supply.

You don't have to bide your time, either, waiting for a
major catastrophe to come along. Listen to these wise, if
playful, words.

It does a heap o' good sometimes,
    to go a little slow,
To say a word o' comfort
    to th' man that's stubbed his toe.
James William Foley

Do you think this is getting a little commonplace? Playing
games, perhaps, with the Sermon on the Mount? Don't
you believe it! Jesus never limited mourning to people
with great griefs. I'm sure he had a kind word for those
who also moaned. Face it, a stubbed toe is pretty important to the one who stubs it. And how much does a
moment of sympathy cost *you*, anyway?

Sometimes a chance to offer comfort comes when you
least expect it. It can be as simple a thing as recognizing
somebody's prop and refusing to pull it out from under
him. I'm talking about security blankets. They come in all
colors, shapes, and sizes. They're called by a multitude of
names. Sometimes they're laughable; sometimes they're
dead serious. But they all have one thing in common.
They give comfort of a special kind.

I want to tell you about an experience I had a short
time ago. I had accepted a job as a daily substitute

teacher, agreeing to take a new class every morning. One day I met Gideon.

He was late to class. He arrived without a word of apology, slamming the door behind him. Noisily, he took his seat in the front row, making a production of opening and closing his desk, dropping his spelling book, and commenting in an undertone to anyone who wanted to listen. Never once, however, did he raise his eyes, even to acknowledge that there was a strange teacher in front of the room.

I placed a worksheet on the corner of his desk, marked him tardy, and went on explaining the assignment. It had looked like the beginning of a good day. Substitute teachers learn to pick up positive or negative vibrations within the first ten minutes, and the feelings I received from these fifth graders had been good ones.

Even when Gideon put his head under the lift-up desk top and stayed there, I didn't sense any trouble. I would give him a few more minutes to settle down, for he really wasn't disturbing anyone. The entire class seemed to have tuned him out. No one watched him. No one responded to his mutterings. I should have recognized the signals, for Gideon was not part of their world.

I was beginning to lose patience when he finally emerged from his desk with a broken pencil in one dirty hand and a bunch of strange-looking objects in the other. At first I thought they were plastic animals, until I saw the round holes in the bottoms. They were rubber erasers, brightly colored erasers, each one shaped like a little elephant. Gideon lined them up on the desk: red, blue, green, yellow. Then he began to move them around, changing places and positions. The work sheet was forgotten, the broken pencil still unsharpened.

"Gideon," I said, "it's time to get to work." He glanced up at me, then looked at his pencil and sighed. "Perhaps it will write better if you sharpen it."

I caught the defiance in his eyes. And there was

something else that should have made me walk with velvet slippers. It was a look of unutterable tiredness, the expression of a child who has gone without sleep. It was a look of deep mourning. But other classroom duties called me, and I put it out of my mind.

When I looked in Gideon's direction again, the pencil was sharpened, but the paper was still untouched. He was rearranging his rubber elephants and muttering softly to himself. I held out my hand. "I'll keep those until you finish your work," I said.

Usually children hand over their playthings, a little grudgingly, but with no ill will. They know they'll be returned at recess. Gideon just stared. I walked over to his desk and reached for an elephant.

"Don't touch that," he said. His voice was perfectly calm.

So was mine. "You're not doing your work," I explained. "Play things are for play time." I started to pick one up, but his hand was over mine like a flash, his fingernails digging into my skin.

"Leave it!" he screamed.

I couldn't have left it if I'd tried. His grip was fierce, and his hands were strong. There was a strange hush in the classroom. I felt sure that something like this must have happened before. Then I struck the spark that ignited the bomb. I reached out my free hand and put it on Gideon's shoulder.

I thought I heard him growl deep in his throat. Then he was on his feet. He pulled back his arm and swung at me, fist clenched, muscles straining.

I ducked in time and caught the blow on my shoulder. Even then, it was enough to unbalance me. He stood there trembling, cramming all four elephants into his torn pocket. "They're mine!" he shouted.

I pointed at the door. There was only one thing I was glad of at that moment. The principal's office was just across the yard, and I could make sure that Gideon went there. We walked rapidly across the blacktop. I reached once for his arm.

"Don't touch me!" he screamed shrilly. And I didn't.

The secretary nodded when she saw him coming. "He's hyperactive," she announced, as if that explained the problems of the world. "He always makes trouble for substitutes," she added. It didn't make me feel any better. I felt oddly defeated as I walked back across the yard and into a quiet, well-ordered class.

At the 10:00 recess I sought out the principal. He was sorry about what had happened, he said. I was not to worry. He would give the boy work papers in his office. He wouldn't be bothering me again.

But he *was* bothering me. The whole thing bothered me. "I wish I'd known that Gideon gets upset so easily," I said. "I might have handled the situation better if I'd realized he reacts this way to substitutes."

He looked at me and shook his head. "Sometimes he reacts this way to his regular teacher. But you're right. Understanding helps. The thing is, we never know if he'll be here or not. He only comes to school when he feels like it." Gideon's mother, he told me, had been married seven times and was currently between husbands. Gideon and his two little sisters were pretty much on their own and were frequently locked out of the house for a day at a time. He took care of them the best way he could, but he was only a boy himself.

No wonder the child mumbled, I thought.

"I really don't know how he copes as well as he does," he told me. "He has so much responsibility, and no one to turn to. He has practically nothing he can call his own."

I read his mind. "The little rubber elephants!" I exclaimed.

He nodded. "That's why he flew into such a rage. He thought you were going to smash them."

"*Smash* them?"

"That's what he said. He claims they're all he owns. He seems to live in fear that they'll be destroyed. Oh, yes . . . there's one other thing you should know. Gideon can't stand to be touched. All of us avoid putting our hands on him, it upsets him so."

He could say that again. I opened my mouth to say as much, then stopped. I knew the penalty for hitting a teacher; something had kept me from telling that part of the story. Instead I said something that surprised myself.

"If it's all right with you, I'd like Gideon to come back to class."

He looked at me, surprised. "It would probably be the best thing for him, if you're willing."

Gideon arrived soon after recess, entering in the same noisy way. The elephants took their places on his desk. His pencil was broken again. I stood beside him and bent over, being careful to keep my distance. He stared straight ahead. He hadn't looked at me since that scene this morning.

"You're welcome in this class," I said, "but I want you to understand something. I'm not going to take your elephants. They can stay on your desk. But I want you to do your work in class and play with them later."

"They're mine!" was his answer. But he reached for his paper and began to write. I was amazed at his abilities. He whizzed through math with little effort, completed his unfinished morning's work, and was ready for P.E. with the rest of the class. I watched him on the ball field. He was good. With a little more nourishment and a pinch of self-confidence he might be *really* good.

Gideon. Such a strong name for a troubled child. I thought of an old, familiar Bible verse.

Thus says the Lord God: "I myself will take a sprig from the lofty top of the cedar, and will set it out; I will break off from the topmost of its young twigs a tender one, and I myself will plant it upon a high and lofty

*mountain . . . that it may bring forth boughs and bear
fruit, and become a noble cedar . . .*   Ezekiel 17:22, 23

Perhaps, I thought, the biblical Gideon had once been
like a tender twig. Perhaps the Gideon who ran across
the field before me had that same chance of becoming a
cedar. But he had very far to go and needed so much
help. I remembered how he'd touched those little rubber
elephants and looked at them with shining eyes. They
were his and no one else's. I wondered if he felt that they
touched him back, for no one else could.

We all have had things that brought us comfort. Our
security blankets, we laughingly call them. We keep them
until we need them no longer, then put them aside, when
we find our own inner strengths.

"Lord, please touch Gideon," I prayed. "In your infinite wisdom, find a way to reach past his fears and let
him feel a hand of love. In the meantime, Lord, please
don't let anyone smash his rubber elephants."

A strange prayer? Perhaps, but God knew what I
meant.

Gideon was the last to leave the room that day. I was
sure he wasn't too anxious to reach home. Besides, he
had to collect his erasers, brush them off, and examine
them carefully.

"Are they all right?" I asked.

"Yep."

I took a chance. "Do you think you might ever use
them?"

He stared at me in disbelief.

"Well, they'd do a good job," I told him. "They're
much better than the little erasers that come on pencils.
They'd be just right for wiping away mistakes. Of course,
that would be up to you."

He hesitated, obviously trying to find the right words.
Gideon was hyperactive, mistreated, hungry, dirty, and
often scared. He was a child in mourning. But he was not

dense. "Mebbe someday. I dunno. But not today," he told me.

Without thinking, I smiled and put my hand on his shoulder. "Today didn't turn out so bad, did it?"

His face was dead serious. "I'm glad you didn't smash my rubber elephants," he said. Then he was gone. It was some minutes before I realized that I had touched him, and he hadn't cringed.

In Gideon's life, the choice was not entirely his. Harshness, derision, unfeeling words, neglect—all these promised to destroy and cripple the precious seed that could have been a pearl. But a caring word, a gentle hand, an understanding voice—these things could give him the time he needed to develop his own inner strengths. Then his shell would open, instinctively, and Gideon would stand alone. In the meantime, his little rubber elephants were all he had.

The lesson is this: every time you reach out to another human being who is in mourning, touch him gently. Don't smash whatever rubber elephants he has. Try to feel his pain and recognize his needs. That's what comfort is all about.

Here's how to polish the second layer of your pearl:

1. Don't be ashamed of tears. They're healing.

2. Let your guard down. Only when you are open and vulnerable can you receive the comfort that is offered.

3. Don't be an island. Be willing to extend a helping hand. Offer sympathy when you can.

4. Never, *never* take away another person's source of strength. Even if it seems useless to you, recognize it for what it is. Have a little compassion and make an offering of your own strength. Do it by talking, by listening, by touching.

5. When you feel that life is handing out too many

thorns, have a good look at the flower that grows at the end of every stem. Read these words:

An apple orchard smells like wine,
A succory flower is blue;
Until Grief touched these eyes of mine,
Such things I never knew.

Lizette Woodworth Reese

Thank you, Father,
for our involvement with each other,
for the ability to feel deeply,
accepting your strength and comfort
when it comes.
Let us walk gently
among men,
reaching out with tender fingers
to touch the rose at the end of the stem.

THREE
THE VELVET TOUCH

Blessed are the meek, for they shall inherit the earth.
Matthew 5:5

Once I saw a poster hanging on an office wall. It was a large caricature of a confused-looking tiger, his striped shoulders hunched, and his tail drooping dejectedly behind him. His brow was furrowed, and the tips of his ears sagged. He had obviously just heard some kind of bad news. As soon as I read the caption, I understood.

"If the meek inherit the earth," he was asking, "what's going to happen to all us tigers?"

He had a point. After all those years of developing what he considered admirable tiger characteristics, was he going to be pushed out of his place in the sun? Was he going to be denied an earthly spot on which to curl his tail? The tiger was extremely indignant, and more than a little worried.

How about the rest of you tigers out there? Does the thought of the meek inheriting the earth shake you up? Does the whole concept seem a little unfair? Do you feel like the ballplayer who discovered that the rules were being changed in the middle of the game?

Don't panic. There is a definite place for your tiger

tendencies, and we'll talk about those in another chapter. Meekness isn't the whole pearl, you know. It's a single quality of character, a luminous layer. But it is the layer we're concerned with right now. If it isn't something you can lay claim to, you'd better get busy working on it.

Already I can hear some groans. The protests are coming in loud and clear. "Who wants to be a pussycat?" "I'm forceful, and proud of it!"

I can also see a certain amount of back-patting. At long last, those of you who never open your mouths think you're going to get what's coming to you. All those years of standing in the shadows are going to pay off. You don't have to move mountains; you don't even have to knock down a molehill. All you have to do is wait . . . until you inherit the earth.

You're both wrong. You're way off the track. You don't understand what we're talking about at all. I'm not sure you even know what the word means. *Meek.* Look it up in the dictionary, why don't you? I think you're in for a surprise.

The truth is, language has a habit of changing to suit the people who use it. Sometimes perfectly respectable words get side-tracked. Occasionally, they get derailed. Take *meek.* At one time it had a fine reputation. It was right up there with gentle, kind, quiet, and tender. A meek person was patient without being spineless. He was humble, without putting himself down. Being meek did not mean being a doormat. It meant having enough self-discipline to keep your cool in times of stress. Today it has become a term of mild contempt, and that's not what Jesus meant at all. He was talking about people who approach life with a velvet touch.

Have you ever listened to a piano that was out of tune? Painful, wasn't it? Being in tune is as necessary for people as for pianos. The man who achieves an emotional balance, a rhythm, between himself and his world is in tune. Izaak Walton liked to talk about the fisherman. Not

the one who fished for his dinner, but the one who fished
for the joy of fishing. "You will find angling," he said, "to
be like the virtue of humility, which has a calmness of
spirit and a world of other blessings attending upon it."

A calmness of spirit . . . a gentle touch.

"That's all well and good," you're thinking, "but what
does all this have to do with inheriting the earth?"

Everything. I'm talking about people who are *able* to
inherit, who arrange their lives so that they *can* "consider
the lilies of the field, how they grow" (Matthew 6:28).
They are not ashamed of taking a ten-minute break.
"Come away by yourselves to a lonely place, and rest a
while" (Mark 6:31). Jesus said the words two thousand
years ago, and he says them over and over to us *every*
single day. We're generally just too busy, or too uptight,
to get off the merry-go-round.

What's that? You don't have time to stop? Take time!
How can I convince you that you can't go through life
with your foot on the accelerator? Occasionally, you have
to pause long enough to see what's going on around you.
Otherwise, life goes by in a flurry and fuzz of sound and
motion. Lights flash. Bells ring. If you're not careful, you'll
be flat on your back in the center ring. You might even
be out cold. If your life is a tornado, you'll end up like
Dorothy. Smack in the middle of the Land of Oz, without
a roadmap home.

To put it as simply as I can, take off your brass
knuckles. I knew an old man who once said, "A wild
stallion doesn't need breaking. He just needs a little
gentling." Have you ever seen a cowboy gentle a horse?
He puts his hand on it, caresses it, sweet-talks it. And the
animal responds. People aren't any different.

The world responds too, if you're patient enough to
'isten, and watch, and feel. The earth is yours, and all its
goodness. All you have to do is accept those riches.

The great thing about this inheritance is that it happens
right now. Our lives, you know, are geared for tomorrow.

We're always waiting for something better around the corner. If we're miserable, it will be better in the next world. Our reward is not this minute, but later.

Wrong! This is where it's at. Life is a gift that God has given. It is to be lived and used. I'm perfectly aware that this is the age of space travel. But in our excitement over finding new horizons, we tend to forget that so far, this earth is the only world we know, and there's a lot of heaven in it.

Elizabeth Barrett Browning said it best:

Earth's crammed with heaven,
And every common bush afire with God;
But only he who sees takes off his shoes—
The rest sit around it and pluck blackberries.

"He who sees. . . ." That's who Jesus was talking about.

Blessed are those who watch. They see white clouds moving behind tall pines. They see soft gull wings making feathered vees against the morning sky. They see the variety of autumn, the mists of winter, the vision of springtime, and the fullness of summer. They notice. They see God in little things.

Blessed are the listeners. They are quiet long enough to heed the still small voice. They hear the message of the wind, and listen to the music of the sea.

"Blessed are you," Jesus is saying, "when you have the calmness of spirit to rejoice in the simple treasures of the earth. When you are patient enough to watch the bird build its nest, quiet enough to hear raindrops on soft grass, humble enough to get down on your knees and see the glory of a spider's web. Especially when you are serene enough to enjoy all these things."

I want to tell you about an aunt of mine, a meek woman, but in the ancient sense of the word. She had a quiet strength, a gentle discipline. She accepted her inheritance without question, and she knew that the rewards were immediate. She could absorb the goodness of whatever season was upon her, and she could look beneath the outer wrappings and discover the gift beneath.

She was in tune.

In my own mind I connected her with springtime, because that's when she had always visited us. I suppose that's why her November arrival seemed so out of character. The hills and fields of our countryside were crisp and dry, and the little lake near our home was surrounded by brown brush and bare-limbed trees, and filled with a stand of pale golden cattail stalks which rustled in the wind like wheat ready for the harvest. Even the sunflowers which grew thick and wild along the path had given up their yellow petals and settled for prickly balls on spindly stems. It had been so lovely a few months before. Now it was barren and dull: nothing you'd want to show a visitor.

The first morning after her arrival, Aunt Kate was ready for action. "How about a long walk in the hills?" she asked.

I reached for my sweater. "I'm afraid it's pretty bleak out there. I've been wanting some flowers for the house, but there's not a sprig worth picking."

She raised one eyebrow. It was the same expression she'd used when I was a child, and she wasn't quite sure I was telling her the truth. "Is that so? I seem to remember that there were plenty of plants last spring. All blooming, too."

"But that was months ago. They've all dried up and gone to seed!"

She smiled at me. "Do you have an old pair of scissors around here?"

It was my turn to raise an eyebrow. But I found the scissors and brought them to her. She reached for the wicker basket, and we trudged together along the rocky path that led away from the house. Dried leaves crackled beneath our shoes; prickly stems scratched our ankles. Aunt Kate stopped now and then to examine a stiff twig or cup gentle fingers around a dried seed pod.

I put an arm around her shoulders. "Never mind," I said, "when you visit us in the spring, the countryside will be beautiful."

She didn't seem to be listening. We had reached the lake, and a light wind was stirring the cattails. "Look!" she exclaimed.

I saw just what I'd expected to see: a lot of dried up bushes. Aunt Kate approached them, wielding her scissors as an artist would his brush. She reached carefully into one bush and seized a long brown stalk bearing hundreds of tiny, dried flower heads. "Steeple bush," she told me.

Snap! I heard the tough stem crack. Aunt Kate pinched it between the scissor blades and guided it into her basket, then moved on. She called the next shrub goldenrod, but you could have fooled me. It looked like a large, yellow spider perched on the tip of a broomstraw. She clipped several. "Such variety," she said happily.

"But they're dead," I protested. "Nobody brings dead flowers into the house."

"They're not dead," she insisted. "They're just dried. Look how perfectly they're preserved. Beauty is more than a pink petal on a green stem. Besides, nothing ever dies that lives to spread its seeds."

She snipped off a milkweed pod. For the first time I noticed that it was shaped like a large teardrop, dark gray, with an etched surface. I began to pay more attention. Each plant had a shape and texture, even a color, all its own.

Yarrow was a golden umbrella, open wide at the tip of a thick stalk. Common mullein was deep mahogany, long and slim, like miniature Italian cypress. Then there were the coneflowers: tiny brown puff balls, each one on a single stiff stem. Baby's breath was as delicate as old lace. Seedbox stalks held miniature lilies, bleached lavender by the summer sun. Queen Anne's lace was a cluster of stars in a web of spun silk.

Aunt Kate even marveled over wild oats, the scourge of the autumn countryside. They were gypsy plants, she told me, untamed and free. Finally, we took off our shoes and waded out to the cattails. They were firm and strong, tall sentinels of the swamp. We picked several and headed for home.

The arrangement she made was a thing of beauty. We put it in a stoneware jug, where it sat without wilting. Once in a while, a few seeds would drop onto the table top . . . gentle reminders of eternal life. Aunt Kate visited us many more times, but I never again connected her arrivals with springtime. It was too limiting. I would think of her and remember instead the lesson she had taught: that things of beauty are often found in unexpected places, when you have the vision to search them out.

If we barrel our way through life at such a speed that we inherit nothing but the wind, we get only an echo of the real thing. The idea is to find some joy along the way. To rejoice in what is at our fingertips. That's what inheriting the earth is all about.

It's a necessary thing to think of the future. It's essential to lay plans for tomorrow. Just don't let the here-and-now get away from you. Shakespeare said that, "No legacy is so rich as honesty." Be honest with yourself. If you're a tiger every day of your life, you'll become so worldly that you'll be no earthly good. So get out that emery board and file down those claws. Every now and then you need to have the velvet touch.

Here's how to polish the third layer of your pearl:

1. Don't be in such a hurry. Take five minutes each morning to claim your inheritance.

2. Next time you're in a tense situation, try the gentling technique. But don't forget to try it on yourself first.

3. Rejoice! The best things in life *are* free. And there's plenty to go around. The bounty of the earth is a little like love: the more that is offered, the more there seems to be in store.

4. Become a student. Become aware. "Speak to the earth, and it shall teach thee" (Job 12:8, KJV). While you're at it, learn the lesson of the earth's generosity:

. . . just tickle her with a hoe and she laughs with a harvest.   Douglas Jerrold

5. When your vision grows dim, and you're sure you're getting a little out of tune, take stock of your riches by reading these words and remembering to say, "Thank you!"

For the beauty of the earth,
For the beauty of the skies,
For the love which from our birth
Over and around us lies . . .

For the wonder of each hour,
Of the day and of the night,
Hill and vale, and tree, and flower,
Sun and moon, and stars of light . . .

Folliot S. Pierpont
Conrad Kocher

Father, we thank you
for the legacy of Now.
Help us to develop
that calmness of spirit
which perceives with clear vision
the treasures
that are found
in unexpected places.

FOUR
CLIMBING JACOB'S LADDER

Blessed are those who hunger and thirst for
righteousness, for they shall be satisfied.   Matthew 5:6

Have you done any dreaming lately? Not the kind you
do when you're asleep. Not daydreaming either. I'm
talking about the kind that lifts you out of the world of
not-a-chance and sends you skimming along the road of
you-bet-your-life.

That's not wishful thinking. On the contrary. It's creative thinking. It's taking stock of where you are and
setting priorities for where you want to be. I suppose
some people would call it planning, but there's really
more to it than that. I call it having a vision . . . and not
letting it get out of your sight.

Let's go one step further. It's recognizing that you need
something which you don't have. And it's wanting to do
something about it.

Jesus said it in even stronger terms. *Hunger* and *thirst*
are the words he used, and they describe pretty basic
needs. They imply action—immediate action—preferably
in a straight line toward a definite goal.

So how's your sense of direction?

Remember when we were children? We sat in class-rooms which had large, colored maps attached to the wall above the chalkboard. The teacher would pull a map down to eye level and tap it with a pointing stick. "Always remember," she said, "that you can't read this map unless you understand directions. North is always at the top; south is at the bottom. West is to your left; east is on the right. It's as simple as that."

And it was, as long as you were reading a map. I soon learned, however, that getting through each day involved two more directions which don't have much to do with compass points. I'm talking about backward and forward.

We ought to be able to tell them apart. We *can* tell them apart. But some of us spend our days looking into a mirror so that we can see only the reflection of what is behind us. What we *need* to be doing is looking straight through the tunnel toward the light at the other end.

It's a matter of focus. When your sense of direction splinters, your arrow doesn't point anywhere at all. You sit on the frayed edges of nowhere and spin your wheels. Your dreams meander, like water in a crooked stream, trickling, without direction, tracing damp trails in dry sand.

You can be as hungry and thirsty as you like, but until you establish that goal and want it so badly you feel deprived without it, you're wandering in a desert of false starts. What you're in for is a case of famine, and slow starvation is a pretty poor way to go.

So let's talk first about the goal. *Righteousness.* No-body's going to argue about the value of that. It's just that the word covers so much territory. Goodness. Morali-ty. Honesty. Justice. Trust. Honor. Love. It's an inspiring word. It implies a well-spent life. It emphasizes a universal truth: that there is in all men the intuitive reaching out for a better way. Psychologists call this effort self-expression. Idealists call it striving toward perfection. Poets call it stretching for the stars. The ancients sent Jason after the

Golden Fleece. David lifted up his voice, and asked for "wisdom in [his] secret heart" (Psalm 51:6).

You can call it whatever *you* like, as long as you understand that it's worth dreaming about. It's worth working for. It's the bull's eye in the target game of life.

So much for the goal. Now, how about the promise? Sounds pretty simple, doesn't it? Satisfaction guaranteed. All you have to do is follow the instructions. I'm going to tell you something that you may not like to hear. *Self-*satisfaction is a dangerous thing. It's first cousin to *self-*indulgence and just a skip and a jump away from *self-*ishness. Real satisfaction is not something you tuck under your arm like a carnival prize. It's something you earn along the way. It creeps up when you least expect it. It's not something you wait for, but something you live with.

Go back and reread the old hymn, "Jacob's Ladder." "We *are* climbing . . ." it reminds us. It doesn't say a thing about reaching the top and stopping. That would be as silly as saying you ate one meal and never needed to eat again.

Don't you see? That's what makes this promise so special. There's no waiting around for results. Satisfaction . . . fulfillment, if you like . . . begins with your first step forward.

Our young son spent a Saturday morning recently working in the yard. The day was hot and humid, and it wasn't long before I heard him in the kitchen, popping ice cubes out of the tray. He put a few in a glass and filled it with water. Then he drank it slowly, obviously enjoying every drop.

"Feel better?" I asked, when he had finished.

He thought about it. "Not really," he admitted, as if surprised. "Of course, I'm not as thirsty now," he explained. "But when it really made me feel good was when it was going down."

So far, so good. Now let's think about hunger and thirst. That's the part that sets us back a little. It's one thing to dream of a better world and to reap the rewards of trying to achieve it. It's quite another to hang in there Monday through Sunday, year in and year out, with your emotions in high gear and your eyes on the big target.

How do you do it? You don't. At least not like that. Unless you're a modern-day Paul Bunyan type, you don't step over mountains. And you don't get paranoid over the realization that you need something which you don't have. You simply put one foot in front of the other and climb the ladder one step at a time. Since we are human beings, we deal with human priorities. We hunger and thirst all right, but we don't have to get hysterical about it. We want to keep the lamp of enthusiasm burning without blowing all the fuses.

Sound complicated? Let me tell you how one woman worked out a way to remind herself what dreams are made of.

My grandmother had two irons. One was shiny and new with an electric cord that encircled it like a soft cat's tail. The other was never used, but it sat on the shelf anyway, right between the Holy Bible and a red geranium plant, which bloomed all year long. It was shaped like a small, cast-iron boat with points at both ends, and it had a lift-off wooden handle which could be carefully removed in the days when irons were heated to indescribable temperatures on large, black stoves. It was heavy . . . oh, was it heavy! But its most remarkable characteristic was rust.

Spreading down its rough sides and over the metal workings of the lift-off handle, rust was like a thin coating of reddish brown icing on a boat-shaped cake. Even the label, which had once stood out along the top rim in bold relief, was encrusted enough to turn my fingers orange when I felt the raised letters.

"Enterprise Iron." You could still read that much . no more.

But it was evidently enough, for my grandmother

wouldn't part with it. Nor would she attempt to clean it. It sat in its place of honor and oxidized quietly. Despite its idleness, it seemed to be an active member of her household.

When she thought I was old enough to understand, she told me the story. "There are three things on that shelf," she said. She pointed to the Holy Bible, the red geranium plant, and the rusty iron. "And they remind me each morning of the way I intend to live out that day."

She took down the Bible and opened it to Matthew. "Man does not live by bread alone," she read, then added, "nor by crisp collars, pleated skirts, waxed floors, smooth curtains, or shiny windows. Those things are nice, and so is a full stomach, but there are other things."

"Like this. . . ." She reached up and took down the geranium. Its leaves were large and healthy, and its blossoms bright. "I feed this plant and water it, but what it thrives on is tender care and sweet talk." Back in those days, most people didn't know about talking to plants. But Grandmother obviously did, and she wasn't a person you argued with. "It pays me back," she said, "by being beautiful. All living things need time for softness, and beauty, and love."

Then she turned to the last thing on the shelf. "That old rusty iron is there to remind me that people are more important than things. Sometimes we get our priorities mixed up and think we're too busy to smell a flower or hug a child. We let our tools become our masters, and all the rust gathers on the wrong places." She held *The Enterprise* in both hands. "This is the place for rust," she told me, "not the human spirit."

In my own kitchen today, I have two irons. One is kept in the cupboard where I can reach it easily when I need it. The other sits on an open shelf where everyone can see it. People stare at it sometimes, for it does look a little odd, right between the Holy Bible and a sprawling red geranium.

I've been told that I should try to clean it, but I won't, for I have better things to do. It is so old and rusty that no one can make out the raised letters on the top ridge. I'm the only one who knows that they spell out the word . . . *Enterprise.*

Enterprise. The willingness to venture out with enthusiasm and spirit. The desire for a better way. The reminder that the place for rust is not on you and me, because people are more important than things. The knowledge that dreams are made up of daily living, with a reachable goal in sight.

Call that goal righteousness, if you like, but remember that achievement is not as important as trying. Reaching the top of the mountain is not as rewarding as leaving your footprints along the way. A sense of direction is vital. But don't worry if you don't get there quickly. Keep telling yourself that it's better to forge ahead and leave a new trail than to meander around trying to follow a dim path.

Have you done any dreaming lately? Go ahead and wish upon a star. Hunger and thirst for goodness, for justice, for love. And when you climb that ladder, find satisfaction in the effort. Let every rung be a new horizon. Recognize righteousness in the scent of a red geranium, the laughter of a human voice. Hunger and thirst after life, and you shall be satisfied twenty-four hours a day.

Here's how to polish the fourth layer of your pearl:

1. Have a dream. Don't let the vision out of your sight.

2. Don't look over your shoulder. Last night's dinner is already cold.

3. Each morning, sort out your priorities. What can you do today that will matter tomorrow?

4. Take pleasure in the joys of living each hour. Remember that Jesus was a righteous man .   . and one who *lived* fully

5. When you need practical guidance, read John Wesley's rule . . . and follow it:

Do all the good you can,
by all the means you can,
in all the ways you can,
in all the places you can,
at all the times you can,
to all the people you can,
as long as ever you can.

Father, we thank you for
holding a bright lantern
at the end of every tunnel.
Give us the wisdom to dream
and the strength to strive,
as we hunger and thirst
for the goodness
that lights the secret heart.

FIVE
TWICE BLESSED

Blessed are the merciful, for they shall obtain mercy.
Matthew 5:7

The English language is very expressive. Words often sound just like their meanings. *Mercy* is a gentle word, pleasant to say and melodious to hear. It suggests compassion. It sings of forgiveness.

Its antithesis is *grudge*.

When I was a child, I read a story about a terrible animal with that name: *Grudge*. He lived on top of a rocky mountain. He was an ugly creature, as unattractive as his name. To top it all off, he had a discontented spirit and, therefore, could never smile. He lived on spite, and he collected ill will. The odd thing was that the story's hero—a small boy named Timothy—was able to defeat the monster with a single weapon: mercy. Timothy felt so sorry for Grudge that he couldn't be angry with him. Without anger, which was the only food that Grudge could eat, the animal became smaller and smaller. Finally, he shrank into a shriveled shadow of complaints and disappeared, eaten away by the pettiness of his own despair.

What happened to Timothy? Why, he grew, of course.

He was strong and healthy. I imagine he was also handsome. And I'm sure he lived happily ever after. All the world loves a hero. Hurrah for Timothy!

Now wait just a minute. Everybody likes stories in which the villain gets his comeuppance. But before we bury Grudge completely, we'd better take a second look at the body.

Look closely. Do you see anything familiar? Come on and face facts. Whether you like to admit it or not, there's a little bit of Grudge in each of us. Nobody is as perfect a specimen as Timothy, because, after all, he's only a paper hero. So be honest, and examine your memory. I'll bet that somewhere in there still lurks an old grievance, something you've never quite been able to forgive . . . or forget. The sad truth is that you may even get a certain pleasure out of remembering.

Victor Hugo understood the feeling. "The malicious," he said, "have a dark happiness." It's a little like having a perfectly good camel's hair coat and wearing it inside out. It keeps you warm, but it also makes you itch.

Don't worry. You're not alone. We all have the completely human tendency to harbor our hurts, packing them away like extra batteries at the back of our mental cupboards, where they promptly leak acid onto the clean shelves.

The character of Grudge, you see, is more than the personification of something bad. Grudge is a good reminder of what can happen to a perfectly good pearl if you drop it into a test tube full of acid. Little by little the shine diminishes, and the layers of beauty are eaten away. Eventually, the whole thing dissolves into a puddle of silt.

If this sounds like a contemporary horror story to you, and you have an overwhelming desire to FORGIVE in one great breath, like making a wish and blowing out all the candles on the birthday cake . . . forget it! You can't do it that way.

Why not? Because you can't climb a mountain, while you're still stumbling over molehills.

That's what petty grievances are: molehills. Stumbling blocks that force you to keep your eyes on your feet instead of your vision on the stars. They pop up and trip you when you least expect it. The only solution is to scrape them out of your way one at a time.

How? I like to call it the system of little mercies. Daily erasures, like the classroom chalkboard at the end of each day. Unless the teacher marks SAVE, everything gets erased. It turns to chalk dust and falls on the floor.

It's time for you to take a lesson from the janitor. Don't mark SAVE around your petty grievances any more. Grind them into dust. Pull them all out of hiding; write their details in big square letters on the chalkboard of your mind . . . then wipe your slate clean.

Now I'm not suggesting that you sit around for days at a time dredging up pet peeves. I can't think of anything more depressing. I *am* suggesting that you use the chalkboard technique as part of your daily living from now on. Give yourself a time limit. Make a bargain with yourself. Say it out loud. "I'll get rid of all of today's grudges before the sun goes down. If I remember any old ones, I'll throw those out too." Don't worry about missing any. Old grudges have a way of popping up again and again. They are tenacious little creatures, ready to fight for their place in the spotlight.

There's only one catch. Your eraser has two sides, just as surely as a dime has heads and tails. They're called *forgive* and *forget*, and if one of them is missing, your daily erasure is just as counterfeit as a one-sided coin. It's fake. Bogus. It won't buy a thing.

I used to have a neighbor. Helen, I'll call her. She refused to forget. She had a grudge and wore it like a badge of honor, resurrecting it daily. She and her sister Anne had grown up in a small town in the Midwest. They both married and went their respective ways. When their parents died, they returned home to settle family business and divide between them a few cherished keepsakes.

Anne took the bone china sugar bowl, and Helen never forgave her for it. She lived near me for several years, and I never drank a cup of coffee in her house without going through the same old routine. First she poured the coffee, then she reached in the cupboard and brought out a cheap plastic bowl. I remember it was plain yellow and faded looking.

"I must apologize," she always said, "for this terrible old bowl. We had a lovely one in our family, but my sister has it. Not that I really mind, of course. She had every right to take it!"

Now, if Helen needed a sugar bowl, she could easily have bought one just as lovely as the one Anne took. But she chose to burden herself with an ugly daily reminder of a petty grievance. She built a molehill right in her kitchen where she could trip over it morning, noon, and night. Worse than that, she kept it alive by talking about it.

Mercy? Not a drop of it. Oh, maybe a little lip service. But that's all. Helen never forgave, because she wouldn't allow herself to forget. She engraved the petty misunderstanding on the chalkboard of her mind in indelible ink. -

Childish? Not at all. As a matter of fact, Helen would have been better off if she'd recovered a few more childish tendencies.

There's an old Bible verse that puzzled me for years: ". . . unless you turn and become like children, you will never enter the kingdom of heaven" (Matthew 18:3). This seemed to contradict everything I believed in. Didn't Jesus tell us to put away childish things? Weren't we supposed to move forward in life, not backward? If innocence was what the verse was talking about, how on earth were we supposed to retain something as fragile as that, and still cope with job hunting, freeway traffic, and daily dishes?

One morning I was carrying the trash out to the curb for the weekly pickup, when I heard noises across the street. Two small boys were rolling in the dirt, pounding each other with their fists. I knew them both. They were usually the best of friends, but at that moment, they seemed bent on destruction. They pulled apart and scrambled to their feet, backing away from each other and throwing insults instead of blows.

The fight was over, but they were still bitter enemies. That's what I thought. I couldn't believe my eyes when I came outside with another basket of trash and saw the same two boys, walking up the street arm in arm. Whatever the difficulty was, it had evidently been settled.

Children are like that. They instinctively know that carrying a grudge means playing all by yourself. They forgive *and* forget. Wait two days, then ask one of those boys what he was fighting about. He'll roll his eyes to the ceiling trying to remember. And he'll probably wonder why you bothered to ask.

Children don't expect life to be a vending machine, in which you insert a coin and receive a chocolate-coated candy bar. Sometimes the score doesn't come out even. But there are ways to deal with petty grievances without letting them ruin the day.

Let me tell you a story.

When our children were very small, we found a green valley on the north fork of the Mokelumne River. We returned, year after year, renting the cabin for a few weeks of happy solitude. Old Jacob was always there to greet us when we arrived. He would stretch his lanky frame into the back seat of the already-crowded station wagon and ride with us as we twisted along the narrow mountain road until we came to the open clearing. He and his wife, Abigail, lived in a small house nearby, caretakers for an absentee owner. They didn't own the cabin, or the valley that surrounded it, but it belonged to them in a way that was unrelated to property deeds.

What was theirs, they shared. So, for a few short weeks each year, the blessings of the little valley were ours, freely given. There was plenty of entertainment, even enough for four active youngsters.

The fat, sassy hog, Bonnie, had thirteen slippery babies. A brown-eyed milk cow stood patiently in a corner of the pasture, while three restless horses flicked their tails impatiently in another. Ripe corn stood tall in the garden; blackberries grew wild along the fence. There were fresh eggs to gather and sour pickles in Abigail's stoneware jar. But the main attraction was the river.

It ran right through the middle of the ranch, gathering speed until it hit the embankment beneath the wooden trestle bridge, then pouring out the other side like ocean foam, slowing and spreading into reedy pools and rocky bottomed shallows. It brought with it whole families of fish, straight from the icy waters of the Sierras. Translucent bluegills, fat crappies, elusive bass . . . but best of all it brought trout, rainbow and brown, pan-sized and delicious.

Our youngest son, Mike, fished for the first time in that river. Jacob showed him how to cast without hooking the seat of his own pants, how to tell when to dig for worms in the compost pile, and when to resort to shiny red salmon eyes, out of a jar with a label on the front. He showed him the value of silence and let him feel the joy of a nibble. But he taught him more than fishing. Jacob told a seven-year-old boy where bird's nests belong.

It was an especially warm summer that year. My husband and I were resting in the shade. The other children had gone wading downriver, but Mike was sitting on a large, flat rock in the blazing sun. He had been sitting there for some time, casting and recasting. Something was eating his bait, but refusing to be caught. It was rapidly becoming a battle of endurance, and I could tell by the way his shoulders tensed that all the sport had gone out of the game.

Suddenly he sprang to his feet and danced on the hot rock. "I've got it! I've got it!" he screamed. Forgetting everything Jacob had taught him, he let out his line too fast and jammed the reel. Throwing down the rod, he grasped the line in both fists and began hauling it in, hand over hand, as if he were pulling somebody up a cliffside. The loose line fell in a tangled mass at his feet. It reminded me of an untidy knitting basket. At the end of the line, suspended midair and dripping river water, hung a gnarled, moss-covered root, the baited hook sunk deep into its soft wood.

Mike dropped it into the dirt and sank down beside it. After a few moments he reached out for the tangled length of line, balancing the snarls in both hands. Angrily, he began to pull, tearing at the knots with his fingers, wrestling the line as if it were a long, skinny snake.

"He's making things worse," said my husband. "I'd better help." But Jacob was already on the way. He crossed the sandy patch at the river's edge and squatted down beside our son.

"Hey, there," he said. "You trying to make a bird's nest out of that fishing line?"

Mike glanced up, surprised, then looked back at the mess he was holding.

"I guess," continued Jacob, "we could clip it here . . . and right here . . . and stick the snarled part up in a tree. That's where bird's nests belong." He paused a moment. "On the other hand, it's a shame to give up on a perfectly good fishing line."

Mike stared at him. "It's not so good," he argued. "It's all knotted up."

Jacob nodded. "Happens that way sometimes. But knots don't mean the end of the world . . . just a little delay in schedule." He held out his hand. "Let's see what you've got there."

Gently he fingered the tangled line, holding it loosely, working the tighter sections apart. "See here," we heard him say, "this loop is like a noose. When you pull on it, it just gets tighter and chokes everything up. You don't ever want to tug on your lines. Remember that. You want to handle them easy and give them room to breathe."

Mike sighed. "Maybe so, but it'll probably take forever."

"What's your hurry?" Jacob grinned. "You've got the rest of your life."

It wasn't long before the two of them, working together, had finished the job. The line was wound, smooth and firm on its reel, and Mike was ready to cast.

"Good luck," said Jacob. He gave the boy a pat on the back. "You'll never have any trouble keeping your lines straight," we heard him say. "Just remember that there's a place for everything, and the place for a bird's nest is in a tree."

I don't remember if Mike caught a fish that day. I doubt if he remembers either. What we all remember is what happened when we arrived home. We were unpacking the car when Mike let out a shout. "Look at this!" he hollered. From behind the wicker picnic basket in the dark recesses of the back seat he pulled out a large, tangled mass of twigs and weeds, dried and brown, held together by a jumble of string and twisted grass. A brief note was attached, fastened to the nest with a rusty safety pin.

"I found this on the ground under the sycamores. I thought I'd send it along to remind you of what we talked about."

Mike stood looking at it, holding it in the palm of his hand. I wondered how much of Jacob's lesson he really understood. After all, he was pretty young. "Why don't you put it on the shelf in your room?" I asked. "It will be something to add to the things you've collected."

But he shook his head. "Jacob wouldn't like that. It's not a souvenir—it's a bird's nest." He headed for the backyard, and I could hear him muttering to himself,

"Gee whiz! You'd think people would know that the place for a bird's nest is in a tree."

The lesson of Jacob was clear to all of us. We gain nothing by holding on to our tangles. Collecting grudges fills the harbors of our minds with dirty water and our mental shelves with clutter. Petty grievances can magnify until they threaten to choke our life lines.

Next time this happens to you, take a moment to smooth your thoughts. Then set your values straight by remembering where bird's nests belong.

Like all the other beatitudes, this one holds a promise. Do you remember Shakespeare's lady "lawyer"? Portia was her name. Wise beyond her years, she understood that mercy acts like a boomerang.

The quality of mercy is not strain'd,
It droppeth as the gentle rain from heaven
Upon the place beneath. It is twice bless'd:
It blesseth him that gives and him that takes.

Mercy isn't the result of reason, or even common sense. It is, at its best, an act of love. It is, at the least, an act of goodness. Luckily for all of us, it takes two giant steps beyond justice: it lets us feel the same relief and freedom of spirit that we give.

How? Simple. You can demonstrate it for yourself in your own kitchen. Start with a cup of cold coffee, the older and staler the better. Look at it. Pretty unappetizing, don't you think? Dark and murky, and filled with sediment.

Pour it out. Dump it right down the drain. Only then, when the cup is good and empty, and rinsed clean, is it ready to be filled with clear, refreshing water.

Each act of mercy, freely given, empties from your cup all the feelings of bitterness, disappointment, antagonism, and resentment that separate you from God. You can physically feel the weight lifted away. Someone once called this phenomenon "that blessed emptiness that leaves room to be filled." And that's exactly what happens. Obtaining mercy *is* being filled with God's forgiving love.

> . . . *forgive us our debts, as we also have forgiven our debtors . . .*   Matthew 6:12

Mercy *is* a boomerang. We forgive, and we are forgiven. While you're at it, run the extra mile and forgive yourself!

The generosity of mercy involves one last step. And it's the toughest chasm to cross. "Love your enemies and pray for those who persecute you . . ." (Matthew 5:44). This isn't a game of pick and choose. "God bless us every one!" said Tiny Tim. Generous words, don't you think? Could you have been that open-hearted? Could you have included Scrooge? Maybe not, but that's exactly what you have to do.

It's so easy to forgive someone you love. It's so tempting to give lip service to the rest. A wise man once said that men only pardon in the degree that they love. That's not the way God works.

Take time out right now, and read these words:

> . . *he makes his sun rise on the evil and on the good, and sends rain on the just and on the unjust.*
> Matthew 5:45

How does that strike you? What does that do to your self-esteem? It's almost a mind-shattering thought that God loves all the troublemakers in the world just as much as he loves you. Unfair? Wait a minute! This is the most generous insurance policy you're ever going to be offered.

Why? Because it includes *you* when you're not at *your* best. That's right. It's a good thing God *is* merciful, for there have undoubtedly been times when you and I have been among the unjust. Did we deserve God's love then? Maybe not. But we got it just the same.

I know. We're only human. Sometimes searching for the spirit of forgiveness is like hunting through an old trunk for something you're not even sure is there. So if you find yourself forgiving those you love, and having trouble finding compassion for the rest, remember these words of Jesus: "Truly, I say to you, as you did it to one of the least of these my brethren, you did it to me" (Matthew 25:40).

Dig deeply for the spirit of forgiveness. Offer it freely. Become one of the twice blessed. And remember: *forgiving* puts you on base; *forgetting* brings you home free.

Here's how to polish the fifth layer of your pearl:

1. Do something nice for yourself today. Get rid of all that extra weight you're carrying around inside. Make a list, if you have to. Write down all your old hurts. Then stand over the kitchen sink and strike a match.

2. Spite is like a spider. It weaves a tangled web. Every single night, wipe your mind clean with the soft cloth of forgiveness. And while you're forgiving, don't forget to include yourself.

3. Remember this: the most meaningful thing we can do every day is to be kind to each other. The rewards are immediate and startling. Kindness turns the tables. It works like music, making harmony where there was discord.

It takes two to quarrel.
It takes two to gossip.
It only takes one to be kind.

4. When someone does something that hurts you, don't compound the injury by sharing it with everyone you see. Discontent is a little like oil. It's easy to spread around, but it clogs the pores of your thinking. Mercy is a song with many verses, but the chorus is hummed softly, to yourself.

5. The ability to forgive is like any other talent: use it or lose it. When you're tempted to backslide, and you need a reminder of how far God's promise really extends, read these words of faith.

Surely goodness and mercy shall follow me all the days of my life; and I shall dwell in the house of the Lord for ever. Psalm 23:6

Father, we thank you for
the gentle gift of compassion.
Give us the insight to
see with generous hearts,
forgiving and forgetting,
and emptying our lives of discord,
to better receive the fullness
of your goodness and mercy.

SIX
IF THE SILKWORM
CAN DO IT, SO CAN I

Blessed are the pure in heart, for they shall see God.
Matthew 5:8

Jimmy's favorite spot in the classroom was as near as he could get to the large aquarium in the corner. It wasn't filled with water and fish, but was spread with clean newspapers and fresh mulberry leaves. Raising silkworms had long been a fourth-grade project, but few children were as fascinated by the little creatures as Jimmy.

He stood on tiptoe and reached into the container with one arm. It was the only arm he had. It was shorter and thinner than usual, and on its blunt stub grew two small fingers. Jimmy was the only person who seemed unaware of the fact that he was handicapped. He had been born that way and had learned to make the best of what he had.

There were times, though, when he was unusually quiet. When he seemed to be apart from the rest of us, working something out for himself. This was one of those times. It was after school, and as I had some spare time, I went over and stood near him. I watched as he gently picked up a fat silkworm with his two fingers and placed it closer to a fresh leaf.

It chomped hungrily, working its head up and down in sweeping arcs, making overlapping holes until the leaf was nothing but a spiny skeleton. At least a dozen of the caterpillars were eating. Creamy colored, fat, and greedy, the little creatures reminded me of miniature bulldozers on the job.

Several others had stopped eating and sat alone, making tentative motions with their heads. I reached out and touched one of them on its smooth, hairless back. It ignored me and continued swaying. It looked almost as if it were trying to draw figure eights in the air. There was a certain grace in its movements.

Jimmy looked up at me and smiled. "It's going to spin," he informed me. "When they stop eating, they're ready to spin."

I nodded. We'd discussed all that in class, but Jimmy always seemed to enjoy repeating it as if it were news. I could feel the excitement in his small body. He'd been waiting for this moment. Suddenly, from the spinneret on the silkworm's underlip appeared a thin, delicate thread of pure silk. The miracle had begun. I heard Jimmy take a quick breath as the thread grew, lengthening and glistening, swaying rhythmically, tracing the movement of the silkworm's body.

"Can you imagine being able to spin pure silk right out of your body?" asked Jimmy. He shook his head, and I heard him sigh. "I sure wish I could do what they do."

"There are lots of different ways you can spin silk, Jimmy," I told him. "And you don't have to be a silkworm to know how."

He nodded. "You're talking about doing your best and improving things around you. I know about that. But I was thinking about the butterfly part . . . you know, about changing from a worm into something beautiful."

I looked at Jimmy's one arm with the two fingers that

he used like tweezers. He seemed so well adjusted that those around him seldom thought about his handicap. But Jimmy, like all of us, wanted to change "from a worm into something beautiful." What could I say that would help? I looked into the aquarium. Soon that silkworm's body would be completely hidden . . . encased in a silk cocoon. It would emerge a changed creature: a gentle, graceful butterfly, preparing to start the creative process all over again.

Surely, I thought, if a caterpillar could spin silk out of its own substance and turn itself into something beautiful, we humans as children of God should have the ability to change coarse living into the fine fabric of life, to transform bitterness into something sweet, to grow, like the caterpillar, into gentler, more beautiful beings.

I turned to Jimmy. "People *can* change," I told him. "Haven't you noticed how they can grow into better people? That's becoming more beautiful, isn't it?"

He watched the silkworms in the aquarium in silence. I knew he wasn't listening. Somewhere among the mulberry leaves was his answer, and he was trying to work it out for himself.

Suddenly his face lit up. "I've got it!" he cried. "It's because they leave their silk behind them!" He stared at me and saw that I didn't understand. "Don't you see? They're just plain caterpillars to start with. But they take something inside of themselves and turn it into silk. That's a pretty good trick, but that's not all there is to it. If they just stayed in those silk cocoons forever, they'd be nothing but dried up worms. But they don't! They come out, and leave their silk behind them, for everybody else to enjoy. They never want it back. That's their secret. That's what makes them beautiful."

His face was shining. Jimmy had found his answer among the mulberry leaves. No matter what his physical handicaps, he was going to be all right. For Jimmy had discovered three steps to the secret of metamorphosis:

(1) Spin a little silk out of the substance of your life.

(2) Leave it behind you wherever you go.

(3) Don't look back into the cocoon you made. Go forward into life and watch the person you become reflect the beauty you leave behind.

Jimmy looked at me and smiled. I saw a beautiful child. I saw a silk-spinner.

Like Jimmy's caterpillars, we can all become more beautiful than we are by spinning a little silk and sharing it. Only then, when we pass it on, can we catch the reflection of its fine, glistening threads. St. Francis knew this secret. "It is in giving," he said, "that we receive."

Beautiful words . . . noble sentiments. But we human beings need specifics. Let's face facts. Caterpillars don't lead very complicated lives. What they do, they do instinctively . . . and that's *all* they have to do. They're never sidetracked by dirty laundry, unpaid bills, and cars that won't start on cold mornings. Granted, they have to survive, but only in the most basic sense of the word. They don't have to make daily, hopefully intelligent decisions.

We do. And, too often, when we've finally finished with the daily essentials of living, what we've managed to spin seems closer in texture to burlap than silk.

How then are we going to clear our thinking? How do we know what God wants us to do with our lives? How do we learn how to spin those threads of silk? Most important, how are we ever going to get to see God?

We can work our way toward the answer in three easy steps. Here they are:

1. Remove your cataracts. How do you go about becoming pure in heart? The same way you go about purifying water. By getting rid of the things that make it cloudy and unfit to drink. A handful of silt doesn't do a thing for your digestion *or* your spirit.

I'm talking about filtering out those things that form cataracts over your inner eyes. *Cynicism, Clutter,* and

Contempt. The three C's of a clouded conscience. Let's look at them one at a time.

A *cynic* doesn't spin any silk. In fact, he doesn't spin at all. He knows it's useless, so why bother? He's had a lot of bad luck, and things aren't going to get any better. Do you know someone like that? He's afflicted with the worst kind of blindness, because he's lost the ability to feel wonder. He doesn't believe in miracles, and he denies himself the luxury of amazement. Thomas Carlyle described him perfectly: "The man who cannot wonder . . . is but a pair of spectacles behind which there is no eye."

Clutter is the backbone of confusion, the spoon that stirs up mixed emotions, the seasoning of dismay. I'm not talking about your house. I'm talking about your life. About honesty and simplicity of purpose. Don't confuse yourself by trying to be like someone else. Fill your place in the sun. Be the person that you alone can be. Look with a clear eye through the cobwebs of choices and recognize the worth of a single spirit. Your potential is already there: God's fingerprint on your soul.

Contempt is a cold wind, blowing harsh and strong and stripping away the fertile topsoil of your content. It slams the door on human relationships. A person who hates spreads unhappiness, like rancid butter on stale bread. His head is clouded, his heart is heavy, and his eyes are closed. Take contempt out of your vocabulary. Try each day to reach out with an understanding heart. Poets call it empathy, but the American Indian said it best:

Grant that I may not criticize my neighbor until I have walked a mile in his moccasins.

Banish cynicism, clutter, and contempt from your life. Know that each day is a new beginning. Look at it with unclouded eyes, and go right on to the next step.

2. Live in the here and now. I'm always amused when I read what Marcus Aurelius had to say about living. "Put an end once and for all to this discussion of what a good man should be, and be one." Hiding in your cocoon is not part of God's plan. Neither is biding your time. The truth is that understanding God's plan for you is uncovered not by sitting around waiting, but by doing.

Sound complicated? Not at all. It's as simple as leaving a little goodness behind you and moving right on to something else.

George Bernard Shaw once said that, "Life is no brief candle. . . . It is a splendid torch." He was talking about the here and now. He was talking about the way you approach daily living. It's your attitude that makes all the difference.

Have you ever tried climbing a long flight of stairs in the dark? Frightening, isn't it? Your sense of balance is gone. You have to feel your way timidly, one step at a time. That's not living. It's treating life like a brief candle that fluttered and went out.

Hold a torch instead of a brief candle, and you'll find yourself spinning silk instead of burlap. Remember that each unselfish thread counts. You don't have to do something spectacular.

If you sit down at set of sun
And count the acts that you have done
  And counting, find . . .
  One glance most kind
That fell like sunshine where it went
Then you may count that day well spent.

                                        George Eliot

3. *Let yourself grow.* Like it or not, we are all in a constant state of metamorphosis. Our tissues and cells are alive. We change constantly. We grow. Life is not a stagnant pond. Human potential is not static. Only by leaving your cocoons behind you do you free yourself

from the attachments that keep you from moving forward to spin silk of a different color and pattern. You are not the same as you were yesterday. That, in itself, is something to give thanks for.

It happened to Jesus: "And the child grew and became strong, filled with wisdom; and the favor of God was upon him" (Luke 2:40). Let it happen to you. Blessed are those who grow in wisdom and stature, who hold before them a splendid torch, who look forward to each day with unclouded eyes, who spin threads of silk from the substance of their lives. They are the pure in heart.

But how do they get to see God? If you think the promise of Jesus involves a glimpse of a bearded monarch on a white cloud—if your vision of God is like that—you're way off base. You're also suffering from a bad case of claustrophobia, because your insight has high walls around it. You're stuck tight in your cocoon, and there's nothing but darkness around you.

Seeing God is not a flash in the dark. It's not a single snapshot. It's more like a steady glow that warms and enlightens. And it involves a lot more than your eyesight.

I once watched a small boy struggle with the intricacies of long division. It was a difficult process for him, and he alternately broke the lead of his pencil and scratched his head. The teacher, in desperation, decided to start from the beginning. Step by step, they concentrated together until, suddenly, something she said flipped the on-switch in the child's mind. His face brightened, and his eyes grew round.

"I see!" he exclaimed.

Nothing had changed in the room. He didn't "see" anything new at all with his outer eyes. But he did understand with that special perception we call insight.

In much the same way we see God by feeling his presence, by recognizing the beauty of his Spirit, by catching for a moment the vision of his plan, by discovering a special purpose to our own lives. We see God when we understand that he has given us, in our human efforts and in our dreams, the raw equipment for Paradise.

God, you see, isn't hiding from us. He isn't standing on the other side of a closed door. And he certainly isn't playing a childish game of hide-and-seek. He is attainable, and he is available. Here and now. In this spot, wherever you are.

How do you feel his presence? Let me count the ways. In the miracle of every living thing, by looking for the best in every man, in the gift of change which is an opportunity for new growth, in the still, small voice that lies deep beneath the surface of you.

With the simple pure vision of a child, Jimmy sought the truth and found the answer among the mulberry leaves. Beauty is found not only in our talents . . . but in the unselfish sharing of whatever we accomplish. Generosity is more than giving away what you don't want. It's giving your all. "He who loses his life for my sake will find it" (Matthew 10:39).

This doesn't mean that you have to go out and die. It means that you have to lose yourself in the willingness to give. Jesus wasn't talking about ending your life. He was talking about making it worth something. The reward? He wasn't a man to mince words. I think he made it pretty clear. Only by giving of ourselves without regrets, with pure hearts, are we blessed with a vision of God's purpose and love.

Whatever their human condition, the pure in heart are never handicapped. They look beneath the rough surface of the oyster. They see the seed of divinity which God has planted in every human spirit. They leave their silk behind them. They never look back.

Does that sound like a pretty big order to you? Perhaps it is. But it helps if you say these words to yourself at least once a day:

"If the silkworm can do it . . . so can I."

Here's how to polish the sixth layer of your pearl:

1. Stop looking at life as a giant tally sheet. Every day spin a little silk in secret, and don't worry about getting credit, for "your Father who sees in secret will reward you" (Matthew 6:18).

2. Put anxiety in its proper place, which is out the back door. Work on one day at a time, and don't let your mind be cluttered with impurities. Worry is like a handful of dirt in an aquarium. It not only makes the water cloudy, but it will eventually kill the fish.

3. Welcome change as an opportunity for growth. Don't slam a door without first seeing what's on the other side.

4. Find your life by losing yourself in living. Light a torch in the darkness. Here's how. Every single day, start out by being honest with yourself. Don't beat around the bush. Choose things to do which will make a difference to another human being. Do them as well as you can.

5. Whenever you begin to feel inadequate, read this quote from Robert Louis Stevenson:

Anyone can carry his burden, however hard,
until nightfall. Anyone can do his work,
however hard, for one day. Anyone can live
sweetly, lovingly, purely, till the sun goes
down. And this is all that life really means.

Thank you, Father, for the inner vision
which lets us look through
the windows of our hearts.
Help us to remember to spin
threads of pure silk,
leaving them willingly behind us,
that the fabrics of our lives may reflect
the glory of your grace.

SEVEN
GETTING IT ALL TOGETHER

Blessed are the peacemakers, for they shall be called sons of God.   Matthew 5:9

Does this seem like a pretty clear-cut statement to you? Read it again. If you think Jesus was telling you to become a pacifist, you're not getting the message. You're not even getting the key word.

Let me explain.

Anyone who has studied languages knows that words often do not translate accurately from one language to another. Certain subtleties of meaning are, unfortunately, left behind. You've heard the expression: "It loses a lot in the translation." Well, it's true, because so often the translator simply has to choose the word in his language which comes the closest, and let it go at that.

That's *exactly* what happened to the word *shalom*. Way back when the Greeks began to translate the Old Testament, they chose the most likely synonym they could find for shalom. It was their own word, *eirene* (ai-re-nay), which meant peace: the absence of war.

In the New Testament, then, *eirene* was used where shalom once would have been used. It's pretty easy to

see how it eventually became translated into English as
peace.

Shalom is a beautiful word. It's one of the most musical
words I know. It hardly needs defining, because the very
sound of it speaks of gentleness and love, joy and beauty.
It is more than a greeting, firmer than a handshake. It
offers a blessing.

I see it as a multifaceted vision, with as many surfaces
as a well-cut diamond, full of light coming from within.
We do the whole idea an injustice if we define it too
easily. Ask almost anyone today what shalom means.

"Peace," everyone will answer. And it does mean
peace. But that's not all. It takes a whole mouthful of
English words to accurately describe the meaning of
shalom. Peace. Well-being. Unity. Balance. God's vision
for perfection. In short: getting it all together.

The Hebrews were so concerned with this total concept
of shalom that they built altars from unbroken rocks and
called them shalom stones. They were trying to express a
harmony, a perfect balance, even in material things.

I'm explaining all this, because I want you to see that
shalom is a *big concept*. Let's try an experiment. Open
your Bible and read Luke 2:14: "Glory to God in the
highest, and on earth peace. . . ." Now read it again,
making a single substitution. Here's what you get:

"Glory to God in the highest, and on earth
shalom. . . ." Can you see the difference? Not just peace:
the absence of war; but shalom: God's total vision for
good spread across the earth.

Do you hear the challenge? Jesus didn't say, "Blessed
are the *peaceable*." He said, "Blessed are the *peacemakers*." Action is implied. Involvement is indicated. The goal
is clear: order out of chaos, harmony out of discord.

Where do we start? Right from the beginning. I'm
talking about working from the inside out, because you
can't tackle the world until you've made peace with
yourself. Shakespeare called it, "A peace above all earth-

ly dignities, a still and quiet conscience." Others call it peace of mind. Label it whatever you like, as long as you realize that it involves a total acceptance of yourself as a child of God.

Unfortunately, there's a fly in the ointment. It hums and buzzes and makes a complete nuisance of itself. It has a well-known name. Anxiety. It's not a harmless pest, for it spreads the germs that cause headaches, heartburn, unhappy marriages, and daily stress. Experts know everything about it, except how to get rid of it.

There is a way to deal with anxiety without reaching, in desperation, for a bigger hammer. The first step is to admit that the threads of our lives aren't always gathered into neat balls, like the ones we used to wind from loose skeins of yarn hanging from a straight-backed chair or looped between the thumb and fingers of two willing hands.

I used to hold the skeins, willing or not, while my grandmother wound the yarn, letting her hands lift and fall, catching the slack as it fell away.

"Hold steady," she'd remind me.

But I wiggled, too eager to be finished, and let the yarn fall, slipshod, from my stretched-out fingers.

"Wait a minute," she'd say then. "Whatever you do, don't move!"

I always remember those words when anxiety rears its head. They remind me not to reach for that bigger hammer. They give me time to look around and take stock. Try it yourself next time you're in a bind. Here are a few things to think about while you're waiting.

1. Be honest. Look at your situation objectively.

2. Don't spend time analyzing your mistakes. It's the most unsettling activity I know.

3. Decide that you are going to solve *only* the most immediate problem first.

4. Find your center of gravity. There is a peaceful place

within each of us that restores harmony and keeps us from tottering. It puts our inner world in balance. Close your eyes and ask for guidance, and you will find it.

5. If anxiety is still with you, channel it. Be anxious to live, not anxious about living.

Now take a deep breath and *act*. Remember this fact: shalom is not static energy. It's found not only in meditation, but in the daily acts of living. Out of each thing we do, out of each new thing we try, we progress further in that thing called Life. And we find shalom, you see, by living.

You are, after all, a human being, not an ostrich. Pull your head out of the sand and look at the needs around you. I don't know whether you know it or not, but you are never really happy in this life when you are thinking of yourself. The only time you get a real glow is when you are doing something for someone else.

You don't have to be an international figure. I'm talking about simple acts of caring. All you have to do is something thoughtful . . . something kind.

Unselfishness is at the heart of a well-balanced personality. So turn your eyes outward. What do you see? A world full of people. Millions of them. Each one with individual talents and individual problems. How can you possibly expect to spread yourself that thin?

You can't. You don't even try. You concentrate on those around you. That's where you make peace. And you let it spread from there.

How do you know where to start? How do you know what to do? I'll tell you one thing for sure. You don't need to go out looking for a problem. Be patient. Sooner or later one will come to you. Let me tell you about something that happened to me. I was in a bind. Peace seemed out of reach. But help came from an unexpected source.

Shawna sat at the low, round table and pursed her lips

as she tried to push the frazzled end of a piece of red yarn through corresponding holes in two pieces of green construction paper. She was making a Christmas stocking, threading the edges of paper together by looping the thick yarn over and under and up again through the holes.

That's what she was *supposed* to be doing. What she was actually making was a mess. Shawna knew it, and so did the rest of the class. It was a simple project, even for retarded children like Shawna, who needed special help. But somehow, the harder she tried, the worse things got. She seemed to be able to force the red yarn through the holes. That wasn't her problem. Her problem was knots. Large, snarled ones that twisted and turned, catching at the holes and tearing the paper. In frustration, Shawna pulled at them harder, trying to make them disappear. Instead of a smoothly laced Christmas stocking, the result was a tangled mess of torn paper and strange, snaggled loops of yarn sticking out at odd angles.

"What am I doing here?" I thought. "I'm not trained to teach a class like this."

My training, at that moment, however, was not the problem. I had been called to teach a first grade class that morning and had been placed, instead, where it was felt I was needed most. They promised me the classes would be small. They *had* to be. I could have refused. I probably should have, I decided. But at the time I didn't know it was going to be so bad.

It was going to get worse if I didn't think of something quick. This school was in the very worst part of the district. My aide was sitting in the corner smoking a cigarette and yelling at the children. Shawna was pulling at her paper stocking, her face getting redder and redder. Despite her learning difficulties, she was able to recognize that her work looked worse than anyone else's. She was seconds away from a real explosion.

Someone at one of the other tables was starting to

pour glue on the floor. I sighed, realizing that this was still the first period of the day. There were five more groups of children yet to come. I had grabbed a handful of paper towels and started in the direction of the glue when the aide tapped me on the shoulder.

"There's too many kids in here this morning," she said. "I don't think we oughta do these stockings."

I turned away from her and looked around the room. There was a scraggly Christmas tree in the corner, decorated with construction paper circles and cardboard stars. On one wall was a winter scene with once-white cotton snow, now gray from being touched by many dirty fingers. The children, sitting around their low, round tables, were holding up their half-finished stockings. One of them, Audrey, let out a long, contented sigh. It was tedious work for her, but she was almost finished. I could see that she thought she had made something beautiful. Maybe it was the only Christmas stocking she would have. Maybe these were the only Christmas stockings *any* of these children would have.

The aide tapped me again. "I might as well go home," she said.

Shawna was beginning to take deep, whining breaths. One little fist began pounding on the table. Nearby, a beautiful white pool of glue was forming on the floor.

"Dear Lord," I prayed. "What am I going to do?"

The answer came. "First things first," were the words that filled my mind. I looked at the aide. "I'm sure you're right," I told her. "You might as well go home."

She looked at me in disbelief. When she left, she slammed the door behind her.

I glanced at Shawna. Everybody else was looking at Shawna too. She was beginning to crush her stocking, smashing it in her fists and tearing at it in anger. I threw a handful of paper towels over the glue and got down to business.

"Look, Shawna," I said, holding out two fresh pieces

of green construction paper. "Let me have your stocking, and I'll give you a brand new one."

She didn't understand. Oh, she heard me all right, and she knew what I said. But she didn't believe me. What she held in her hands, though a mess, was hers. If she gave it to me, she'd have nothing. She started to scream.

I felt a tightness in the back of my neck like a long knot that stretched clear across my shoulders. No one else paid much attention after the first shriek. It seemed that the class was accustomed to Shawna's frustrations. I tried to put my arms around her, but it was like offering comfort to a thrashing machine. I was amazed at her strength. I knew instinctively that this tantrum was going to last a long time unless I figured out a way to stop it. After all, the tension had been building up in her all morning. Silently, I cursed a situation that gave children things they couldn't handle and teachers who couldn't handle *them*.

I was helpless against her fury. It seemed that I had two choices. I could bundle her up and carry her out of the room, or I could work out some solution right here in the class. Either way, I couldn't do it alone. I needed help, and I asked for it. You don't sit down and close your eyes and pray in a situation like that. You speak directly to God.

"Help," I said. "I need you to show me what to do."

Almost immediately two small brown hands were thrust in front of my face. They held a long piece of smooth, unknotted red yarn. The hands were Audrey's.

She motioned to the green paper stockings that I had dropped on the floor. "Shawna has to let her knots hang loose," she said.

Wonderingly, I picked up the paper and put the two pieces together. Shawna was still screaming and pounding, and now she was kicking out at everything in sight. The little table rocked under the onslaught. But I didn't need the table. All I needed now were my two hands and faith.

Very slowly and deliberately, I began to pull the yarn through the holes, holding it out so Shawna could see it each time I was successful. Then it happened. The yarn knotted. My neck knotted too. I pulled impatiently with moist fingers.

"Not that way," urged Audrey. "Let them hang loose, like this." She took the knotted section and jiggled it loosely in her fingers, pulling the pieces apart until I could see exactly how to unravel it. The knot came apart easily, and I pulled the red yarn through the hole.

Did I imagine it, or were Shawna's yells getting further apart? I threaded the yarn through another hole, pulling it slowly, letting the ends dangle. Why hadn't I thought of this myself? I'd always known the trick of pulling a knot free in all directions instead of yanking it tight.

Audrey put her head over my shoulder. "That's right," she nodded. "I don't think you'll get into any more trouble now."

Shawna's screams had stopped altogether. So had the pounding. I thought she must be exhausted, but she just sat there, hiccuping softly, watching my hands.

After a while, she reached out and took the paper from me. Audrey moved close to her. "Put it through the hole," she said. "That's right. Now remember, Shawna, to let your knots hang loose."

I took a deep breath. The tightness in my shoulders was gone. Somehow I was going to get through this day. Audrey jiggled the yarn, smoothing away a potential problem. I watched Shawna. She was still hiccuping gently, but through a happy smile. She was working all by herself now. Instead of the tense, unhappy child she had been a few moments ago, I saw a little girl making a Christmas stocking . . . *peacefully.*

I learned something that day. Peace is contagious. It's like a river that flows smoothly through a dry valley, quenching the thirsty land. It requires positive action. Just standing by doesn't solve a thing. But it also requires guidance. Here it is:

A new commandment I give to you, that you love one another; even as I have loved you, that you also love one another.   John 13:34

Let your outstretched hand be a prayer for peace. Let it reach out in an act of kindness, in a favor for a friend. Take time to listen. Be willing to serve. Every time you help someone else get his act together, you add another note to the harmony of the song within yourself.

Recognize yourself as God sees you: created in his image. Stretch out your hand for shalom the way a child on a swing reaches out for the sky, with joy and excitement. Call yourself a child of God, and accept his blessing:

The Lord bless you and keep you: The Lord make his face to shine upon you, and be gracious to you: The Lord lift up his countenance upon you, and give you—shalom.   Numbers 6:24-26

Here's how to polish the seventh layer of your pearl:

1. Accept the challenge. Start with yourself. Let your own knots hang loose. Banish anxiety from your vocabulary. "In quietness and in trust shall be your strength" (Isaiah 30:15).

2. Acknowledge that the world is constantly changing. This is not always good and not always bad. The important thing is that you make the necessary adjustments and keep on growing . . . like the pearl has to do within the oyster. Sometimes it becomes necessary to change gears. That's not important. The important thing is that we keep moving forward.

3. Remember this: it takes more courage to declare peace than to declare war.

4. Think about these four qualities of character. They'll help you get it all together:

   1. Faith: Make your peace with God.

   2. Firmness: Face life with a clear head.

   3. Fortitude: Hang in there!

   4. Flexibility: Hang loose.

5. Don't wait for tomorrow. Start today. And don't forget to ask for help. Read this prayer of St. Francis:

Lord, make me an instrument of your peace.
Where there is hatred, let me sow love;
Where there is injury, pardon;
Where there is doubt, faith;
Where there is despair, hope;
Where there is darkness, light;
Where there is sadness, joy.

Thank you, Father
for the music of the universe,
for your vision of harmony
that flows like a river
through our lives.
Give us the courage
to follow the currents of your love
seeking the everlasting goodness
of shalom.

EIGHT
THE EYE OF THE WIND

*Blessed are those who are persecuted for righteousness'
sake, for theirs is the kingdom of heaven.*

Matthew 5:10

In my part of the country, we have seasonal north
winds. *Santanas,* we call them. They arrive without warning. They come with great force, blowing hot and dry.
Tumbleweeds roll across roads and pile high against
country fences. Tension mounts, and tempers fray. Dust
devils play across fields, suddenly changing direction and
exploding into millions of breathless pieces. The santana
sings its own peculiar song: a lusty howl that rises and
whistles, then falls to howl again.

Just as suddenly as the santana comes, it is gone. The
change is dramatic, and it is always predictable. It is a
stillness—almost a sigh of relief. Then sensation bursts
the seams of silence. The very air is alive, and so clear
that I can reach out and trace the mountain shadows with
my fingertips. I can press my face against the clouds. I
can see through God's blue sky all the way to eternity.

The santana is a harsh wind. But the rewards are worth
the trouble.

Standing up and being counted is a little like undergoing a spiritual santana. The reward? A peace that's alive with feeling. The ability to see with your heart. A clear day in the climate of your life.

Isn't that exactly what Jesus promised?

Sure, but sticking your neck out isn't always easy, and it isn't always fun. Do you long for the quiet life? Are you tired of daily problems and hourly friction? Do you want to sit back for awhile and feel nothing but a zephyr, as you watch the rest of the world go by?

We all feel like that now and then. That's why we need to take an occasional five minute break. It relaxes and refreshes. It restores our strength. But that's all it does. Retirement doesn't breed courage.

Aesop, that wise storyteller of ancient days, liked to remind us that it's easy to be brave from a distance. It's also easy to be brave when you're one of the crowd.

Do you know anything about coyotes? They are prairie wolves. They move in packs. Their only strength is in numbers. They keep a safe distance from other animals, and come out at night, crowding together as they hunt for food, yipping defiantly to show their fearlessness.

It's all a lot of humbug! Let one single coyote become separated from the pack, and he stops, right where he is, puts his nose in the air, and howls unhappily at the moon. Face him head-on, and he turns and runs, his ears down and his tail between his legs. He's only brave at a distance . . . and when he's one of the crowd.

That may be all right for coyotes, but the easy way is not always the best way for the rest of us. Difficulties are not solved by standing back. One of the most powerful messages I ever read was hand-printed on a piece of construction paper and hung above a chalkboard in an elementary classroom.

I always wondered why
Somebody didn't do something.
Then I realized that I am
Somebody.

Who are *you*? Where are you going to get the courage to be *somebody*? What do you do when fear reaches out and threatens to swallow you whole? Listen . . . it's time for a story.

The "eye of the wind" is a common nautical term. It means, simply, facing into the direction from which the wind blows. But it didn't mean that to me as a child. I saw it, in my mind, as a huge eye that could see everything, especially me. When the wind blew, therefore, I was a goner. That eye was aiming directly at me, and its breath would blow me away to some terrible place, far from my family and friends.

When my sister told me that she'd read somewhere that the wind had teeth too, it only made matters worse. What the eye wouldn't do to me, I reasoned, the teeth would take care of.

It was an unfortunate coincidence that these were depression years, and my mother had taken to serving for breakfast what she liked to call hot cereal, and what we knew was really mush. It was terrible stuff, not at all like the hot, creamy cereals we have today. It was cooked forever in a large saucepan on the back of the stove. It was thick, and it was slimy. No amount of butter, sugar, or cream would make it go down.

"If you don't eat, you'll starve," my sister assured me. It seemed highly preferable. Anyway, I wasn't really worried. I was going, that morning, to the house next door to see the elderly man who was affectionately known in the neighborhood as Uncle. We were scheduled to play Chinese checkers while his wife, logically called Auntie, fried fresh doughnuts. I was in no danger of starving.

The only danger I faced was between our house and theirs. Because a March wind was blowing, and that meant its eye was out there somewhere, waiting.

My sister must have read my mind. She was the only one who knew my fearful secret. "If you don't eat your mush," she whispered, "I'm sure you'll blow away."

I eased out of my chair and stood by the front window, watching. The fact that I went out the front door at all was a real tribute to the drawing power of hot doughnuts and Chinese checkers. I got across our yard and into theirs without too much trouble. But my heart was pounding, and I kept my head ducked so as not to see that eye.

I had reached the middle of Uncle's lawn when a terrible whining sound filled the air. It was, I knew, the wind whistling through its teeth. My skirt blew over my face, and I staggered, caught in the gust as it whipped around the corner of the house, pushing swirls of loose dirt before it.

I reached out desperately for something, *anything*, to save myself, and touched the smooth bark of a young walnut tree. It had been planted the year before and wasn't much bigger than I was.

To me, however, it seemed like the staff of life, and I clutched it tightly, wrapping my arms and legs around it. It swayed, and I swayed. I must have also done a good amount of screaming, for Uncle suddenly appeared by my side. He put his arms around me and waited a minute.

"Whatever are you doing?" he asked.

"Holding on," I sobbed. "I-I'm scared."

"Of what? Surely you're as brave as that little twig you're trying to climb. Just look at it. The wind blows it almost down, but it springs right back and carries you along with it."

I was a little ashamed, but not enough to let go.

"It doesn't know about the eye and the teeth!" I shouted.

Uncle was wise enough not to ask me what I meant. He just nodded. "Probably not," he agreed. "That's the difference between trees and humans." He paused. "Do you want to know why this tree is so brave?" I didn't, but he kept right on. "It's because it can breathe."

"*I* can breathe!" I insisted, wondering why he didn't try to save me. Here I was in mortal danger, and he just talked.

Uncle shook his head. "You can breathe *out*," he told me. "That's different. What you've got to do now is breathe *in*."

I couldn't. I was crying too hard again, and all my breath did seem to be going in the wrong direction.

"Just a tiny little breath, to start," he urged.

I hiccuped loudly. "That's fine," he smiled, "but not so loud."

I smiled back and took a breath.

He took his arms away and stepped back. A terrible, whistling gust of wind tore around the side of the house. I opened my mouth to scream, but Uncle stopped me. He didn't say a word, just planted his feet far apart, lifted his arms straight out with the palms facing up, threw back his head, and *breathed*. I was reminded of the picture of Moses in the big family Bible. From that moment on, in my mind, Uncle was a man of God.

"You can do it too," he assured me. "And you can let go of that tree. You won't be afraid anymore, and I'll tell you why. March air is full of courage. Just look at what it's doing, if you don't believe me."

I looked around. I believed him, all right.

"When you take a big breath of courage," he went on, "it fills you up inside. Courage is very heavy stuff. You couldn't possibly blow away if you were filled with courage. Well . . . could you?"

I shook my head. Very gently he pried my small arms from around the little tree. "Now then, we'll do it together." And he held my hand and showed me how to stand, like him, with my arms raised and my head thrown back. Together, we *breathed*.

I think now it may have been my first real breath. It filled more than my lungs. It went clear to the tips of my outstretched fingers. Courage was, to me, a newfound thing, and I was surprised to find that it smelled a little like fresh-cut grass and early roses.

Uncle released my hand, and I stood alone. The rushing air pushed back my hair and washed my face. My skin tingled. I swayed a little, but I didn't blow away.

Uncle had been right. I believed it then, and I know it for a fact now. Courage is very heavy stuff. It makes you able to look right into the eye of the wind.

For a long time after that, I connected courage with deep breathing. Then one day I read these words by Friedrich Hegel:

What you can become, you are already.

And I knew what Uncle had known all the time. The potential is within you. Sometimes it just needs a little activating.

A lot of us, unfortunately, are habitual shallow breathers. We may be made of good stuff, but it never comes to the boiling point. Take a deep breath. Fill your lungs and feel the difference. Activate yourself. Start living with your head held high and your shoulders thrown back.

For goodness' sake, don't worry about where your strength is going to come from. It's already there, waiting to be used.

How do you know you'll be successful? You don't. But you'll never know what you can do until you try. And I can promise you this much:

Mankind has a will to survive. Read that sentence again. Say it out loud. Believe it, because it's true. There is a basic urge deep within each one of us that keeps us coming back for more. Hope is contagious, and herein lies its strength. It adds to the weight of courage . . . which is already very heavy stuff.

Now that you know you've got it . . . what are you going to do with it? Here are three ways to make your tiger tendencies work *for* you:

1. Have the courage to be an example. Whether you like it or not, that's what you already are. Listen to what Nathaniel Hawthorne had to say.

*Every individual has a place
to fill in the world,
and is important in some respect
whether he chooses to be so or not.*

He was talking about daily living . . . and it takes a certain amount of courage to deal with that.

Santanas are *not* daily occurrences. They're strong winds—Goliaths, if you like—and they demand a special kind of courage. I like to call it a joint effort, because it's a fact that we don't have to face our Goliaths alone.

Whenever I think of facing a problem that seems overwhelming, I remember that wonderful story of a young boy who stepped out in front of the crowd and faced his challenge. And I remember that David didn't tackle Goliath all by himself. How do I know? I have it on the best authority. ". . . lo, I am with you alway, even unto the end of the world" (Matthew 28:20, KJV).

Why did he tackle Goliath at all? It's a thing called responsibility. "Whatsoever your hand finds to do, do it with your might" (Ecclesiastes 9:10).

Oh, but that was a long time ago. In the age of heroes. Is that what you're thinking? Poppycock! *Every* age is the age of heroes! The Westward Movement isn't over, you know. There are new horizons in our everydays. There are trails to blaze in our tomorrows. A life without goals is like a bird who never flies. He has wings, but because he's content to stay on the ground and eat worms, he never knows what it is to soar.

So go ahead and fill your place in the world. Stand up and be counted. However difficult things seem, whatever troubles you're facing, put your face into the wind and meet them head-on.

2. Have the courage to keep your mouth shut. It's a sad fact that a blow-hard doesn't really accomplish anything but a lot of breathing *out.* When you spend your life tooting your own horn, you really don't have time to do anything else. Let your actions speak for themselves, then let it go at that. You may not like hearing this, but I'm going to tell you the truth. No one really wants to hear about your battle scars. John Donne knew this, and he said it in a way you may want to remember.

I have done one braver thing
Than all the Worthies did;
And yet a braver thence doth spring,
Which is, to keep that hid.

3. Have the courage of restraint. Know when it's time to keep your hands off. You have to learn to have a certain amount of respect for the rights of others. You can't go around walking all over people, even if you are convinced that your way *is* best. This isn't courage. It's interference.

Here it is in a nutshell: you have to learn the difference between what you *want* to do and what you *ought* to do. Sometimes it takes a lot of courage to stand back and watch. I saw a wonderful example of this kind of self-control. Let me tell you what happened.

I was driving along a country road one day, when I automatically took my foot from the accelerator and pushed the brake pedal, straining to see what was in the road ahead of me. The small round object didn't move. It could have been a leaf or a rock, but it wasn't. I had barely avoided crushing a baby bird!

Still soft, with downy gray on its feathers, it sat like a stoical soldier facing the dangers of an unexplored world. It made no attempt to move.

Before I could open the door, I realized that the tiny

creature wasn't alone. With a long, squirming worm held firmly in her beak, the mother bird circled and landed, dangling breakfast just within reach. The worm hung, suspended, then disappeared into the gaping mouth. The mother flew up into a heavily-leafed maple. I could hear her nervous, twittering sounds growing gradually more insistent. The young bird lifted his head and raised one wing experimentally, Then, apparently changing his mind, he settled back, opened his beak wide, and waited.

There was nothing gentle about the mother's voice now. It came out like a squawk, as she spread her wings wide and dropped to the grass beneath the tree. Deftly she plunged her beak into the sod, braced herself, and pulled. Another worm, longer and fatter than the first, twisted wildly, hanging like a living corkscrew in the air. She lifted herself with outspread wings and glided toward the fledgling. But she didn't land. She swooped and hovered, letting the food hang, tantalizingly out of reach.

But he refused to be tempted, so she dropped it with an impatient plop into the open mouth, then flapped her wings rapidly, circling and returning, again and again, as if to say, "I've done my part. Now it's up to you." Her song now was plaintive, distressed, and I could see why. The baby made two tentative hops and ruffled his feathers, but decided to stay, head up, beak open, making harsh, demanding sounds.

Just like a child, I thought. As long as you do everything for him, he'll never take a step on his own.

But she didn't approach him again. She gathered her feathers closely about her like a soft cloak and settled down to watch. I could sense her torment as she forced herself to keep her distance. At first there was an occasional persuasive chirp as she sidestepped nervously along the branch. Then she was quiet, keeping her watchful vigil alone.

Should danger appear, she would be ready, but she

was playing the waiting game. She had a lot more self-control than I would have had.

The fledgling couldn't believe what was happening. I could tell by the way he kept opening his beak. When no food came, he puffed himself up and gave a few impatient hops. For a while he sat motionless, then let out one shrill peep after another. She saw him, and she heard him, but she didn't make a move. This time she didn't even answer.

Frantically, the young bird lifted his wings and spread them, fluttering wildly. Nothing happened. He gave two or three short hops, then tried again. This time he fluttered several inches above the ground before he fell. His progress was slow and jerky and not always in a straight line, but he finally made it to the side of the road.

He rested a moment, then lifted his wings and rose several feet in the air. Apparently astounded by what he could do, he flapped wildly, trying to stay up. When he almost touched the ground, he soared again, this time reaching the branch where his mother sat alone. She turned her head and buried her beak in the feathers of his neck, ruffling them gently. That was all she had time for.

Heady with courage, he left the branch, catching a current of air and swooping effortlessly to the lawn. With quick, sure jabs he pushed his beak deep into the soft, moist grass and came back holding the top half of a long worm which seemed to stretch, then snap into one unbroken piece, like a thick rubber band.

I wanted to applaud. As he flew high with his breakfast into the upper branches of the tree, I looked again at the mother bird. It seemed to me that her chest was swollen with pride. Why not? What better time to be pleased with your children than when they finally spread their wings and fly?

I thought of my own family and felt a little ashamed. I had been doing unto others for so long that I'd forgotten that there were things they could best be doing for themselves. By taking care of all their needs, I had been clipping their wings.

What wisdom God gave to the smallest of creatures! Surely he would also teach me the rules of the waiting game. I released the brake on my car and headed for home. It would take a lot of courage on my part, for I had some fledglings there who were just dying to spread their wings and fly.

Now I know what you're thinking. What does all this have to do with persecution? Let's face it. We're not all going to be martyrs. Anyway, I don't think that's what Jesus was talking about at all. I don't even think that's what he wanted. But he was a pretty good student of human nature, and he knew that men and women are pretty quick to criticize each other. If you don't think this is a form of persecution, then you'd better open your eyes and look around you. It was a wise man who shrugged his shoulders and said, "Oh, well, you can't please everyone."

Believe me, he had the right idea. He knew that you can be criticized for doing too much, and you can be criticized for keeping your hands to yourself. But he also knew that it wasn't important as long as he did the most important thing of all: *his best.*

"Throw fear to the wind!" said Aristophanes. Like Uncle, he knew that courage is right where you need it. Whether your Goliaths are personal problems or community crises, whether you face a zephyr or a santana, be true to your convictions. Stand *out* when you stand *up.* Your reward is a clear conscience and a peaceful heart.

Here's how to polish the eighth layer of your pearl:

1. Learn how to judge your actions. Ask yourself this question: Are you going to do something today that will make a difference to another human being?

2. Watch for the wind of opportunity. Go right out and stand in it. Take a deep breath and look life in the eye.

3. Be an example . . . but be a quiet one. Let your actions speak louder than your words.

4. Pray for the wisdom to know when it's time to stand back. Have the courage to occasionally play the waiting game.

5. Remember . . . you're not alone. You don't have to face your Goliaths all by yourself. Read these words:

Have courage for the great sorrow of life and patience for the small one; and when you have laboriously accomplished your daily task, go to sleep in peace. God is awake.

Victor Hugo

Thank you, Father,
for walking beside us
as we face the winds
that blow across the days of our lives.
Teach us to breathe deeply
of the breath of life;
let us accept each challenge
with open eyes and steady hearts.
Make us worthy, Lord,
of your kingdom.

NINE
THE SALT OF THE EARTH

You are the salt of the earth; but if salt has lost its taste,
how shall its saltness be restored?   Matthew 5:13

The human condition is something unique and special.
The human potential is infinite . . . as vast as the grains of
salt which fill the sea, and lie untouched beneath the
earth, and pervade our very being.

That's right. You *are* made of salt, at least part of you.
It's in your sweat, your blood, your tears.

It's not really a food, you know. Your neighborhood
druggist calls it sodium chloride; the grocer calls it common table salt; a gourmet cook refers to it as seasoning.
However you want to label it, its value is indisputable.
Without it, none of us would live for very long; it is
absolutely essential to our existence.

Grains of salt. Little white crystals. Rich in legend and
history. The oldest article of trade in the ages of man. Salt
has been used for money in nearly every country of the
world. It keeps food from spoiling. Among the Hebrews,
salt symbolized purity, quality, steadfastness. Men who ate
salt together could never be enemies. It is one of the

earth's natural treasures. It even adds flavor to the food we eat.

There isn't any mystery in Christ's message to us. "You are the salt of the earth. . . ." Those are words of love. "You are special people," he was saying. "You are something precious."

The admonishment that follows is just as clear. Don't lose the joy that was yours at birth. Don't lose your zest for life!

It's a danger we ought to be aware of. That's why Jesus made such a point of it. Going stale is an everyday phenomenon. Look around you and count the ways. Bread gets moldy; apples get soft; potatoes sprout long, crooked eyes; milk separates and turns sour . . . and people lose their enthusiasm for living. Don't let this happen to you! Guard against becoming one of the has-beens.

Listen to those words again. "You are the salt of the earth!" He was talking to you and to me. I don't know why you should be so surprised. Kings and presidents don't make the world go round. People do. People who get up in the morning and do the things they have to do. People who work, and play, and laugh, and cry, and suffer, and rejoice . . . and are still willing to get up the next morning and do it all over again.

Sure, we need leaders. But even more, we need real human beings. I'm talking about the people who are always there when you need them. They recognize opportunity and act instinctively and speedily. They are compatible with God's will without being sidetracked by pomp and circumstance. They are the beautiful people, full of flavor. They are . . . the salt of the earth.

When I was a child, we had a neighbor whose name was Grace. But everybody called her Auntie Brown. It suited her, for she was probably one of the plainest women I've ever known. She knew it, and did little to change her appearance. Her hair was cut short and combed straight back, making one deep wave over her right eye. She wore no makeup except for a bit of hasty powder and a shadow of rouge when attending church every week and the Women's Club once a month.

Auntie's hands were rough and, when she grew older, as brown and gnarled as the bare root roses she bought early each spring. She had a prominent nose, but no sense of smell. She'd lost it sometime in her middle age, she told us, and she was constantly throwing open the back door and asking, as she put it, for someone to "step in here a minute and sniff." It was no trouble for me. I was always hanging around nearby, looking for an excuse to visit.

"See here now," she'd always start out. "Is there something burning in this house?" Or, "Did I go and put too much toilet water on myself?"

I always answered no to that one, no matter how sweet she smelled, because I couldn't imagine why she wanted to wear toilet water anyway. Sometimes she'd say, "I've got company coming. Just walk around and see how this place smells."

Once she'd seen a skunk running under the high front porch and had hung garlic down there to chase it away. The skunk left, all right, but afterward she couldn't tell whether she smelled like the animal or the garlic. When she saw our faces, she knew.

I was glad I hadn't lost *my* smell, because without it I would have missed out on a childhood full of homemade doughnuts. The aroma left her kitchen like the proverbial beckoning finger of fragrant smoke, searched me out and found me wherever I was, then led me, panting with anticipation, to the black wood stove and the white sink lined with crumpled paper towels. As far as I remember, she only made one kind of doughnut. Plain cake. Probably she iced them and sprinkled them with sugar, but I never waited to find out. She gave them to me hot, so that I held them gingerly, blowing on my fingers and nibbling at the brown crusts. Did you read Chapter Eight? Auntie's doughnuts are the reason I braved the wind on a cold autumn day.

She had good timing; I still associate hot doughnuts with crisp, cool, windy, autumn air . . . and fresh grape juice with hot summer days.

The grapes grew in purple bunches as big as wisteria clusters, clinging to a little lean-to arbor in the backyard. She squeezed them and bottled the sweet juice, dispensing it in tiny jelly glasses with an ice cube on the hottest days in August.

Auntie didn't have a yard; she had a garden. Every spare inch of soil was devoted to something living. The only places where nothing grew were Uncle's work shed, which held his carpenter shop upstairs and a white enamel bathtub in the middle of the laundry downstairs, the garage, and the front walk. The rest of the space was sprouting, budding, blooming, ripening, going to seed, and fallowing . . . but not for long. Sometimes the garden hopped and chirped, for there were also rabbits and chickens. Uncle sold off the rabbits for profit, but the chickens were for eating.

He was a gruff man, but he didn't have it in him to chop off a head. Auntie did. She'd send him in the house and get it over with. I watched her get it over with hundreds of times. It was the highlight of my day. Later I thought it had been a backward kind of arrangement. Auntie, who grew living things, standing by the stump holding an axe, while Uncle, who cut things up all day in his carpenter shop, had to look the other way behind a closed door.

"You do the things you have to do in this life," she told me. "It isn't always easy."

She taught herself to play the violin after she was sixty. That wasn't an easy thing to do, either, she told me, but it was another of those things she had to do. Not quite in the same category as chicken heads, but a necessity for her, nonetheless. I heard someone ask her why she decided to learn the violin so late in life.

"Why not?" was her simple answer. "Nobody was stopping me."

She believed it was never too late to teach an old dog new tricks, and she had the old dog to prove it. He was named Zippy and was the living example of Auntie's philosophy. She taught him new tricks almost every day. Either he was a very bright dog, or Auntie had been right all the time.

Auntie was an educated woman, an avid reader, and first on the spot with the neighborhood news. But she was not a gossip. She'd simply tap at my mother's kitchen window and say, "See here, have you heard . . .?" Then she'd get back to whatever she was doing. She was there when we needed her, whether it was for a pot of hot soup, the use of her wood stove when our more modern conveniences broke down, or a hot mustard plaster when she heard one of us cough. I even remember one time when she appeared with a bottle of horse liniment. I never complained of aching muscles again.

Auntie was also a honky-tonk piano player. I'm sure she never realized it, because her repertoire consisted mostly of hymns, the older the better. But she pounded them out with a wonderful abandon and staccato touch that would have made any self-respecting player piano hang its head in shame. Her music rang out daily, loud and clear, filling the neighborhood air. No one before or since Auntie Brown has made me want to dance to "Onward Christian Soldiers." Occasionally she'd ripple through "Narcissus" or "Country Garden." Maybe that's why, for years, I thought they were hymns without words. There was only one explanation for her style. She loved the old songs, and she played them with spirit.

That's the way she lived. With spirit. If you had met her, you might have called her a character. But that's not quite right. She *had* character, and there's quite a difference. She was the salt of the earth, and she never lost her flavor. She was a plain woman on the outside. But when I was a child, I saw her with a special sight, and I knew that she was beautiful.

In those days we had never heard of the Jet Set. Being rich and famous and, therefore, beautiful was an analogy that made little sense. "Pretty is as pretty does," my mother reminded me. And I believed her. It never occurred to me until many years later that beauty is a three-letter word.

Joy!

Without it, it's a pretty plain world. Joy adds a twinkle to your eyes, a certain vitality to your voice, a spring to your step, and a dimple at the end of every smile.

We used to sing an old hymn of celebration that told of the ". . . joy, joy, joy, joy . . ." down in our hearts. Remember that one? It's a happy song, but it only tells half the story. According to the words, all that joy is down in our hearts to *stay*.

Wrong! Joy is like an arrow. It isn't very useful if it doesn't go anywhere. It needs direction. Down in your heart is a good place for joy to start, but why do you want to keep it to yourself?

Does this mean that you have to go around laughing all the time? Of course not. But it does mean that you have to start living! And this involves more than getting up in the morning and making the beds. It means living with a zest for life. It means being an active, caring human being.

The example was set two thousand years ago, when the greatest Teacher made a joyous commitment to life. His enthusiasm was contagious; his lesson was simple. It is just as true today. A man's wealth is measured not by how much he has, but by how much he gives. In the joy of giving is your strength. It is the only food that satisfies your spirit. It is the only spice that flavors your life.

Have you ever seen a daisy chain? It's a lovely tradition at graduation ceremonies all over the country. Outstanding young girls, symbolizing honor and purity, carry an unbroken chain of white flowers. I hate to jump from daisies straight into mathematics, but the daisy chain is, I think, the perfect example of the truth that the whole is greater than the sum of its parts. One flower alone may be beautiful, but when many are linked together into a thick, unbroken chain, then passed from one human hand to another, until the circle is complete, there is more than a chain of daisies. There is harmony and strength. There is a giving, a receiving, and a passing on.

I never see a daisy chain without thinking of the old Danish proverb that says,

He who gives to me . . .
    Teaches me to give.

I'm reminded of my friend Sally. She arrived at my door one day with a large, old-fashioned dishpan in her arms. It was brimming with bright, ripe cherry tomatoes. Their red skins were shining as if she'd polished them, and some still wore fresh green leaves like proud caps.

"Can you use a few of these?" she asked.

"*Can* I? You've just solved my salad problem for tonight." I got out a bowl and started to fill it.

"No, no!" she protested. "Take them all. I have plenty more!"

"But, Sally," I protested, "there are so many. At least let me pay you for them."

She laughed and patted me on the shoulder. "Haven't you heard?" she smiled. "There are some nice things left in life that you don't have to pay for. That's what these are. Volunteers. They didn't cost me a cent, and I'm passing them on to you the same way." She pulled me by the arm. "Come on. I'll show you."

Together we walked along the road to Sally's house.

There had been a large barren area at the side of the back lawn where she had been struggling for years to get the grass to grow. Now it was covered with masses of green vines and leaves covered with tiny red miniature tomatoes.

"I came out one morning, and there was a single little plant starting to grow. Before I knew it, the vines were creeping in all directions. They've already dropped seeds in several places and started over again. I can't tell you how much we've enjoyed them. It's like receiving a gift whenever we come out here to pick some. Probably it's my imagination, but it seems like they're the sweetest I've ever eaten."

A little breeze sprang up and rustled the leaves. The red balls stirred and swayed; they seemed as alive as tiny people in scarlet coats. Like an army, they prepared triumphantly for a march across the lawn. Unlike other armies, they asked for nothing but an occasional drink of water and a little sunlight.

"Aren't they something?" Sally asked. "You can't put a fence around anything that full of life. You mark my word. Before long, they'll find a way to travel."

I went home and thought about those little volunteers. It was comforting to think that there were still some nice things in life that didn't require payment. Sally had always been a volunteer herself, giving freely of her time and love. Maybe that's why they chose her yard for a sprouting place.

They might be growing at Sally's, but for the rest of the season, I found that they wouldn't leave me alone. Every time someone called to ask me to add one more project to an already busy day, I looked at the bowl of tomatoes which Sally found such pleasure in replenishing, and I found it hard to say no. If Sally could only spread her supply far and wide, I thought, the world would be full of volunteers.

The amazing thing was that when I volunteered happily

and willingly, the work didn't seem to sap my strength.
Ordinary household chores and family duties didn't make
me sigh with boredom. On the contrary, I seemed to be
able, like the tomatoes, to produce plenty of energy and
enthusiasm for the job at hand.

It was not, however, until early the next spring that I
realized the full potential of giving. I was standing by my
kitchen door, drinking a cup of coffee and enjoying the
cool, clean air of early morning. There was a small,
brick-edged plot of ground near my mint bed that had
been weeded and prepared for planting. I hadn't decided
what to grow there. Herbs, maybe, or a sunny patch of
marigolds. I no longer had the choice. One tiny plant had
reared its head. I looked closely. It was a volunteer
tomato.

Sally had been right. The seeds of giving had found a
way to travel. A few weeks later I was overwhelmed with
tiny red fruit. They seemed to delight in producing faster
and faster. They had more energy than my family could
possibly absorb.

One morning, while I was stripping the vines of a new
day's crop, I glanced across the road and saw our new
neighbor struggling with a carload of groceries and four
small children. She looked tired and sounded cross. I
remembered how, when my children were younger, I had
often felt the same way. There had been too much to do,
and not enough time. What I'd needed then, I thought,
was a neighbor like Sally, who would have taught me
that the only true gifts are of yourself and given freely.
That a task accomplished voluntarily and with joy is not a
task at all.

I looked across the street again. Surely there was a
vacant spot somewhere in that yard just waiting to be
filled. I smiled to myself. The seeds of giving do find a
way to travel. Sometimes they need a little help from a
human hand. I watched my neighbor herd her children
into the house. Then I went to look for a dishpan.

"He who gives to me . . . teaches me to give." The words are true, but the seeds of giving must fall on fertile ground. How do you manage this? Follow these rules:

1. Accept. You do this by tilling your soil. Turn it over and let the sun warm it. Make it receptive to the seed. It's not hard. All you have to do is stop protesting. Learn to say thank you for what you have. Count your blessings. Don't be afraid to be grateful. It's not painful at all.

2. Enjoy. As the seed bursts and lets the young plant reach up toward the sunlight, so should you let yourself feel that same freedom and happiness. Reach out toward life with your hands spread wide, so you can feel the sunlight on your fingertips.

3. Share. Whatever your seeds of living produce, the bounty is yours to give. Reap the harvest of yourself, and realize the full potential of all you have to give. Read this Basque proverb: "God is a busy worker, but He loves help." Now turn to Luke 22:27 and read: "For which is the greater, one who sits at table, or one who serves? Is it not the one who sits at table? But I am among you as one who serves."

There's nothing dreary about salt, and there's nothing dreary about you! Because you've learned the secret of seasoning. Live and give, and do both with joy. That's the way to put foundations under dreams.

Here's how to polish the ninth layer of your pearl:

1. Give away a piece of yourself every day. Don't ask, or expect, to be repaid. Don't think about what you're going to get; think about what you're going to give.

2. Act instinctively. Don't take your time, or you might miss your chance. Someone once said, "You cannot do a kindness too soon, because you never know how soon it will be too late."

3. Remember the daisy chain. Don't let yourself become the missing link.

4. Accept, enjoy, and share. Give thanks every morning for a new beginning. Don't be a wader. Jump in with both feet.

5. When you're tempted to become sidetracked by pomp and circumstance, read these words and keep from being derailed:

This time, like all times,
is a very good one,
if we but know what to do with it.

Ralph Waldo Emerson

Thank you, Father, for the knowledge
that every day is worth living,
for the awareness of the rapid heartbeat
of a living world.
Let us reach out with eager fingers
to feel the pulse of life.
Let us taste anew
the flavor of each sunrise,
as we look with joy
at the vision of a pearl.

TEN
YOU CAN LIGHT UP A LIFE

You are the light of the world . . . Let your light so shine before men, that they may see your good works and give glory to your Father who is in heaven.

Matthew 5:14, 16

It's impossible to see in the dark. But it's amazing how many of us try. We move slowly, without direction, groping and stumbling. We are short-circuited and don't know what to do about it.

The answer was pretty obvious for one small boy named Johnny. He was sitting at the dinner table with his family one stormy night. Suddenly there was a loud clap of thunder, a flash of lightning, and all the lights went out. Nobody moved. The entire family sat for a few seconds in surprised silence. Then Johnny's voice came out loud and clear.

"Don't just sit there," he exclaimed. "Somebody strike a match!"

Go ahead and laugh. I know it's a funny story, but there's a lesson to be learned from it. Darkness is alien to the human spirit. I'm not talking about the dark of night,

which is a blessing: a time to rest, to restore your ener-
gies, to trim the wicks of your subconscious so your spirit
won't flicker.

I'm talking about gloom. That heavy cloud that settles
like thick smoke over your thoughts and casts dark shadows over the mirrors of your minds.

Alien or not, it seems to come. When it does, we react
just like the family at the dinner table. We sit there. We
can't seem to get our act together. We can't even remember where we put the matches.

What happens is a little like standing on the sidelines of
life. You're cut off from the action. You've been benched.
There's a heavy cloud hanging over your head, and the
mirror of your mind is made of nonreflective glass.

That's exactly the way Mary Thompson felt. A few
years ago she told me her story.

She sat quietly in church one morning. She was in the
front row, and it made her uncomfortable. There was
nothing between her and the altar, and Mary felt as if she
was right out in the open where everybody could see her,
especially God.

But she didn't want to be seen. She'd wanted to hide,
she told me later, because she was such a failure. Oh, she
used to be a lively, energetic person . . . a real go-getter.
But one misfortune after another had made the spark go
out of her life. Things seemed pretty dismal these days.
She felt as if she were feeling her way through a dark
alley with a blank wall at the end.

She shouldn't have come this morning. She wasn't
worshiping. She was acting out a charade. But the familiar words were comforting to hear. She forced herself to
listen more closely. She used to be able to repeat those
verses by heart.

For now we see in a mirror dimly, but then face to face.
Now I know in part; then I shall understand fully, even as
I have been fully understood. So faith, hope, love abide,

these three; but the greatest of these is love.
1 Corinthians 13:12, 13

Mary sighed. She didn't like looking in the mirror these days. There was nothing worth seeing. She glanced up above the altar at the pastel patterns in stained glass. They were dull, too, this morning, for it was a cloudy day, and there was no sunlight to make them shine.

Then she caught her breath. A single bright ray of light shot through a strip of golden glass and divided, sending long, misty beams in straight lines to the altar. The single candle caught the light and held it, reflecting in its halo the multicolored beauty of the window.

Mary watched the light fade. But the little candle continued burning brightly.

She didn't listen to the sermon. Her mind was electrified. For a brief second she had been that candle. She had looked in a mirror darkly, then face to face, and caught the reflection of light. It was as if someone had raised the blinds so she could see out the windows of her house again. To her surprise, it was daylight.

"You did not choose me, but I chose you . . ." (John 15:16). Mary searched her memory for the words and found them. She knew they were true. Even when she felt her world was darkest, God had shown her a ray of light.

When she let her gratitude flow back to God, it was like flipping the master switch. She'd learned an important lesson. In order for any light to continue burning brightly, its fuel must be replenished at regular intervals. The source of her supply was so simple.

I am the light of the world; he who follows me will not walk in darkness, but will have the light of life. John 8:12

"*You* are the light of the world. . . ." What a compliment! What a vote of confidence! What a challenge!

Jesus was no procrastinator. He didn't say, "Tomorrow you *will* be the light of the world"; or even, "You *can* be the light of the world if you try harder." He said, "You *are* . . . right this minute. I have already turned on the switch."

There's some pretty basic psychology involved here. It's called the theory of *you are what you think you are.* And it can work in two directions.

I once watched a mother and her young daughter walk through a crowded store. They were both carrying packages. The child was overloaded. Her little arms were stretched around a large bag, and she had another sack looped over one arm. As they passed me, I heard what her mother said.

"Be careful when we come to the door. Let me go first, and I'll hold it open. For goodness' sake, don't drop that box!"

They came to the door. The mother held it open, and . . . you can guess the rest. The little girl dropped everything and fell down besides.

No one had told her she was clumsy. No one had said, "You're going to fall." But the tone had been explicit. The expectation had been: *failure.* And that's exactly what happened.

A depressing story? Of course it is. But wait a minute. Don't you remember that I said this theory can work in two directions? Let's take a look at Molly Nelson. She was a rather plain child. But Molly never knew it. "You have a beautiful smile," her mother said. "You have an interesting nose. Your hair shines like silk." Molly blossomed. She smiled her lovely smile; she wrinkled her interesting nose; she held her shining head high. I knew her when she was a young woman, and Molly walked in beauty, because that's the way she felt.

How do *you* feel? Have you been putting your lamp under a bushel? Do you sometimes feel like it's going to flicker and go out? Remember this: You *are* the light of

the world, and your fuel supply is an ever-ready source.
But God isn't going to pour the oil into the lantern for
you.

Look into a fireplace and watch the flames. They leap
and dance. They are alive with dreams and hopes. A pile
of logs sits on the hearth, but somebody has to be willing
to place them on the fire.

Try these rules for replenishing your inner candle
power:

1. *Let faith flip the switch.* It's the strongest medicine
that I know of. It isn't something vague in the back of
your mind either; faith makes things happen.

Now you may think that it's sun and water, but I know
for a fact that faith is the active energy that sprouts seeds.

My grandfather was an orange-grower. He believed in
good trees, good soil, irrigation, and fertilizer. But most of
all, he believed in God. I used to follow him when I was
a child. I'd tag along behind him, following his footsteps
through the furrows. At the end of the day he would say,
"I've done all *I* can!" There was never a negative note in
his voice. He took good care of his trees, but he was only
the junior partner. He depended on God to do the rest.

He felt the same way about the large vegetable garden
that he planted on a piece of clear land. He prepared the
soil carefully, hoeing straight furrows and dropping the
seeds in even rows. "We'll have vegetables in the
spring," he said. And we always did. To me it was like a
miracle—all those green plants sprouting from hard little
seeds and producing enough food for several kitchens.
But to him it was as natural as the sun coming up every
morning and spreading its warmth like a soft blanket,
reaching into dark corners, and polishing the air with the
light of day.

Faith *is* natural. It is the bridge we cross to things
unseen. It is the candle that lights our way.

2. *Light up yourself with hope.* Start out with the
physical you. Start every day with a smile. Let your joy

come through. If you don't feel joyful . . . pretend. No, this isn't living under false pretenses. It's pulling yourself up by the bootstraps.

It was Alexander Pope who said that, "Hope springs eternal in the human breast." In simpler terms, hope is what keeps you and me from lying on the mat and letting the referee count to ten.

My husband once counseled a man (Jim Peterson we'll call him) who was unable to smile. He was a gentle man, but if you had met him on the street, you wouldn't have believed it. He was large and rough looking. He'd had a hard life, and it showed.

"I look mean," he said. "I know I do. I've got a wife and eight kids to support, and I can't get a job, because I scare people."

He was right. My husband looked at him and thought he would be easy to pick out of a police line-up. He was the prototype of the Hollywood villain. But telling him so wasn't going to help matters.

My husband hesitated, then said the only complimentary thing he could think of. "I'll bet you have a nice smile." He wasn't prepared for the man's reaction.

Jim lowered his head. "I can't . . . do that," he muttered.

"Do what?"

"I can't smile. Believe me, man, I really can't."

"Can you try?"

"You don't understand me, man. This face doesn't smile. I don't remember if it ever could. My muscles don't work that way."

My husband looked at him in disbelief. Jim's face was very expressive. He could frown; he could scowl; he could speak clearly. There was nothing at all the matter with the muscles in his face.

"Look, Jim," he said, "you don't have to force yourself to smile. You don't even have to know how. All you have to do is let the good feelings inside of you come out."

Jim shook his head sadly. "That's easy for you to say. I've got lots of good feelings. But they're stuck in there. Ain't no use tryin' to change things. I can't help the way I look."

This was no time to argue. "OK," my husband said, "let's work on those good feelings and forget the rest. Here's what I want you to do this week. Every time one of your children makes you feel good, I want you to *imagine* a smile. Don't bother about your face muscles. Don't even think about them. All you have to do is smile on the *inside*. Can you do that?"

Jim nodded, but he obviously thought this whole procedure was a mighty roundabout way of getting him a job.

When he came back the next week, he looked the same as ever. He took off his knit cap and sat down. He looked rough, tough, and . . . yes, he still looked mean.

My husband smiled at him, hoping for some kind of response. Jim crossed his arms and stared back. His mouth was beginning to twitch. "This was about the worst week of my life," he muttered. "My face is all sore."

"What happened?"

"Well, you know how you told me to smile on the inside whenever my kids made me feel good? Listen! I've got a big family. Those kids of mine made me feel good most of the week!"

"What does that have to do with your sore face?"

Jim made a queer sound deep in his throat. He tucked his head a minute, then looked up at my husband. "I'm surprised at you," he said. "You ought to know that when you fill something clear up to the top, it has to come out."

My husband looked across his desk. He had been right all the time. Jim Peterson was a man with a beautiful smile . . . as soon as he let his joy come to the surface and overflow.

Jim Peterson was a man who was down and out. But

he learned to light up his physical self. It wasn't long before he decided he wanted to get off the mat before the count of ten.

You can do the same. Light up *your* life with a smile. Remember that laughter originated with God. With the blue sky for his lens and a quickly passing cloud for a shutter, he must look down and be tempted to say, "Smile, you're on candid camera." Learn to look for the gentle humor around you. Laugh at two robins tugging at the same worm; at little autumn leaves that curl and snap their stems, then float to the ground . . . free at last. Recognize the wink of a laughing eye. See the light side of a heavy situation.

When no one seems to appreciate your efforts, cheer up. Mark Twain once felt the same way and gave this lighthearted bit of advice:

Always do right.
This will gratify some people and astonish the rest.

Laugh softly, and laugh heartily. "Your hearts will rejoice, and no one will take your joy from you" (John 16:22).

3. Have a little self-confidence. Your talents are unique. Use them; don't abuse them. If you're a timid starter, take a tip from Lao-Tzu and know for a fact that

the journey of a thousand miles begins with one step.

If you feel inadequate in today's world of computer technology, tell yourself that men are more important than tools. If you don't believe me, prove it by putting a first-rate tool in the hands of an incompetent workman.

Borrow some words from Abraham Lincoln and say them out loud every single day. "I am not bound to win but I am bound to be true. I am not bound to succeed but I am bound to live up to what light I have." This is good works. You are bound to do the best you can.

There is something about you that is different from any other human being. Don't be afraid to be *you*. Go ahead and reach for that star. Who knows? You may be taller than you think you are.

4. *Light someone's path with kindness.* Compassion is a candle with a strong wick. I don't know whether you know it or not, but being a good Samaritan is not out of style. Human beings need other human beings. Vincent Van Gogh said that, "The best way to know God is to love many things." I think he should have included people.

Don't be afraid of depleting the fuel for your lantern. A long time ago I read a Russian proverb that said, "There is more light than can be seen through the window." So feel safe in spreading yourself around. Be generous with your time. Pretend you're a star and poke a hole in someone's darkness. Just think what it would be like if we all acted like good Samaritans every day of the week. Shakespeare's words would finally ring true.

"O brave new world; that has such people in it!"

Here's how to polish the tenth layer of your pearl:

1. Accept the gift of light. Know that it is good.

2. Take stock of your abilities. Have you been keeping them a secret? Pull them out of mothballs and let them go to work for the Lord.

3. Be kind to someone every day. You don't have to be a Girl Scout. Just be a good person.

4. Take a tip from a Chinese fortune cookie. Don't curse the darkness; light a candle.

5. Have faith in God, hope for the future, and love for your fellowman. If you feel a spell of darkness approaching, remind yourself that:

The sun comes up every morning . . .
It hasn't failed us yet!

Thank you, Father,
For faith:
the key of trust
that opens closed doors;
For hope:
sweet expectation,
the strength of dreams;
For love:
the great commandment,
the light of the world.
Grant us peace, that we may listen,
wisdom, that we may understand,
and joy, that we may reflect
the light of your love.

THE LAST LAYER
THE PEARL OF GREAT PRICE

Errors, like straws, upon the surface flow; he who would search for pearls must dive below.   Ovid

Something elusive about the pearl has always captured the human imagination: its luster; the glow that seems to come from within. Perhaps we admire it because it is created by a living creature.

You're a living creature too. Have you taken a good look at yourself lately? I'm not talking about seeing a reflection in the mirror. I'm talking about diving down beneath the surface, and taking stock of the inner you.

How are your natural resources holding up? Are you confronting life and reacting with faith, hope, and love? Or are you still indecisive, unwilling to take the plunge? In short, are you held back by doubt?

Cheer up! It was Galileo who said, "Doubt is the father of discovery." So you had better stand back . . . there is nothing more exciting than a human being who is beginning to discover himself!

It's a little like exploring a new continent. It's a lot

easier if you have a roadmap. And you do! You have a whole set of guidelines.

The miracle of the Beatitudes is that Jesus recognized our strengths and weaknesses. He also recognized the unique human capacity for sympathy, for love, for pity, and for understanding. He knew our need to reach out, one man to another, and offer something of ourselves. He knew these things well, because he lived as one of us.

Don't you see? He is describing those qualities that are common to mankind. All of these traits are part of the pattern of living. They're facts of life. We don't plan on being poor in spirit. Sadness isn't something we particularly look forward to. But these things do happen, and we're stronger because of them.

Some of the traits take a little effort on our part. Most of us have to work at slowing down and being quiet enough to let our senses absorb the treasures of the earth. We have to learn to breathe before we can stand up and be counted. We have to have patience. We have to have the perspective to realize that every single action we take has a reaction. Each unkind act diminishes the whole. Each hand reached out in friendship spins a little silk.

Does it seem to you that some of these ideas overlap? Indeed they do. They are related, one to the other. They touch, just like the layers of a pearl.

The well-rounded personality, you see, is formed a little at a time, building and overlapping through a living process of change. The result is what we call character.

One shining level of existence is not enough. It's shallow—it has no depth. That's why Jesus didn't stop with the first Beatitude. He *knew* how many facets of ourselves we have to develop before we become like the pearl of great price.

There is an old legend that says that the pearl is a gift from God. But I don't think so. The potential is God's gift. The effort has to be our own. Because you *are* a child of God, you have inherited the bounties *and* the responsibilities.

Does that seem like a pretty big order to you? It is. But happiness is the by-product that you receive along the way. The Beatitudes are like a song of celebration, extolling the human spirit and its potential.

The pearl is in the oyster, constantly growing and developing. The seed for the pearl of great price is within you. How you react to the challenge of everyday living determines how well that pearl grows . . . and glows.

God meant for you to glow. He meant for each one of us to shine with a unique and individual beauty. Use the Beatitudes as a guide; take your talents and stretch them until they reach a new dimension.

And remember this: it's true that something elusive about the pearl has always captured the human imagination, but Jesus has made it possible for the human imagination to capture the pearl. Reach out for it now. Claim your inheritance and accept your challenge.

". . . where your treasure is, there will your heart be also."   Matthew 6:21